Square in a Square®

Diamonds by the Square
REFERENCE BOOK
VOLUME TWO

by Jodi Barrows

The Square in a Square® system
allows quilters of all skill levels to produce
complex patterns with accuracy and ease!

Contents

Introduction 3
Supplies 4
Techniques 5
FAQ 6
Finishing 7
First Things First 9
Ruler Instructions 10
4-Patch & 9-Patch Sizing 13

OPTIONS
Basic Square Option 1 16
Option 2 17
Option 3 - Flying Geese 18
Option 4 - Half Square Triangles . 19
Option 7 - Basic Diamond 20
Option 11 21
Option 14 22
Option 18 – Canadian Geese 23
Option 19 – Long Thin Triangles 24
Option 20 – Roof Tops 25
Option 21 26
Option 22 – Diamond Twist 27
Option 23 – Diamond Pineapple   28
Option 24 – Wagon Spokes 29
Option 25 – Long Legged Ladies 30
Option 26 33
Option 27 – Seven Sisters 34
Option 28 – Looking Glass 36
Option 29 – Instant Star 37
Option 30 – Father Goose 38
Option 31 39
Option 32 – Slim Jim 40
Option 33 – Snowball 41
Option 34 – Halloween Eyes 42
Option 35 – Jodi's Favorite Corner 43
Option 36 – Rooftop Triangle ... 44
Option 37 – Granny Goose 45
Option 38 46
Option 39 – The Trumpet 47

CHARTS
Option Sizing 50
Diamond Charts 67
Measurement Charts 68
Diamond Block Building 72

INTERMEDIATE PATTERNS
Crossroads 85
Postage Stamp Star 88
Blaze 91
Cathedral Star 94
Poinsettia Star 99
Fringe Flower 104
Star Frost 110
Pathway to the Stars 114
Crown of Thorns 117
Sassafras Tea 120
Kaleidoscope 123
Spinning Stars 126

Special Thanks:
To my quilting friends and family, thank you is not enough. You continue to be a huge support and I couldn't do it without you. You are all great, precious people.

Quilt Piecing, Pattern Testing Proofreading and Support:
Janie Alonzo, Janet Blazekovich, Cherie Blocker, Carol Daniels, Melinda Davis, Paula Doll, Kristi Droese, Mary Ann Edens, Rita Hardman, Kathy Kuryla, Mary Lumbard, Karen Morrison, Annette Pulido, Kay Roberts, Janet Scheer, Jenny Singleton, Elaine Stanley, Rhonda Stephenson, Bonnie Taylor, Cecilee Wilson, Bonnie Walker, Peg Oppenheimer, Helen Ray, Jean Kearney

Hand and Machine Quilting:
Cheri Blocker, JaLonn Carter-Stanley, Elaine Stanley, Kathy Kuryla, Jodi Barrows

Office Support:
Steve Barrows, Jenny Singleton, Elaine Stanley

Graphic Design:
scottcornelius.net

Photography:
scottcornelius.net

First Printing, Copyright © 2015 Square in a Square®

All rights reserved. No part of this book may be reproduced or transmitted in any form or by any means electronic or mechanical, including photocopying, recording, or by any information storage and retrieval systems without permission in writing from the publisher. Copyright laws strictly enforced.
ISBN-13: 978-0-9882432-9-3

Introduction

Welcome to the Square in a Square® way of constructing quilts. For over 25 years, I have been creating quilts using this system. Now it is time to teach you the power of these new diamond units. You will love them and probably be a little upset with me for holding out all these years!

The beauty and ease of these new units using the Square in a Square® technique continues to amaze us! The speed and accuracy of these normally difficult, thin triangle units are unbelievable. To think, these are supposed to be unattainable designs now made so spectacular!

Watch the movement in these quilts when using the diamond shapes as they add so much dimension and depth to your designs. These once hard patterns that fall into this speedy, fun and accurate category truly excite me. I can't wait for you to catch this excitement and experience the feeling of creating "hard" patterns so simply.

This diamond reference book is Volume Two of the Reference Book encyclopedia series. Volume One is the Square in a Square Reference Book with the square Options #1–#17 with Volume Two containing 23 diamond Options. These books are created to work together, although they do stand-alone also.

The 23 diamond options expand the possibilities to an endless number of patterns. From these diamond units, quilts can now be made with ease, accuracy and speed. No more "y" seams, set-in pieces or ripping out again! The diamond center expands your ability to create circles and curves, movement, depth and dimension to simple strip piecing. Difficult quilt designs are a thing of the past when you understand this simple technique.

I recommend learning the basics of the square which are Options #1, #3 and #4. Then, taking that knowledge and learning Options #7, #18, #19, and #20 of the diamonds. Powered with those skills, you are ready to tackle almost any design in the quilt world. This concept of simple strip piecing turns any level of seamstress into a Master Piecer!

With its easy to follow patterns, multiple block sizing and page after page of endless charts, this Volume Two Reference Book will keep you at the sewing machine.

WE'RE HERE FOR YOU

You will never be left to fend for yourself while learning the system. We have a growing collection of instructional videos on our website that are available anytime, day or night, and always free! Visit us online at **squareinasquare.com**. If you need further assistance, don't hesitate to call or email. We are always happy to help and to answer any question you have about the system! Call us toll-free at **888-624-6260** or email us at **info@squareinasquare.com**.

I hope to see you down the patchwork path!

Blessings,

Jodi

Supplies

Fabric
Use 100% cotton, quality fabric. Yardage denoted in patterns is the actual amount with small cutting errors.

DO NOT prewash your fabric. You will find that piecing is more accurate with sizing in the fabric. If you are concerned about the colors bleeding when washed, test a small sample and treat as necessary. If you choose to prewash your fabric, use spray starch as you press the yardage.

Rotary Cutter and Mats
All the patterns in this book are cut using a rotary cutter and a self-healing mat. Always have a sharp blade and a good size mat. If you are serious about quilting, you should consider having multiple sizes of mats to use with different sizes of fabric.

Rulers
You will need an accurate acrylic ruler with clearly marked measurements, including ⅛" marks. You can use the original Square in a Square® ruler or the smaller R5 Square in a Square® ruler. The Square in a Square® rulers were specifically developed to make cutting angles a breeze.

4- and 9-Patch Crosscut Rulers
Some of the patterns in this book may call for cross cutting single strips or sewn strips of fabric. Aligning the Square in a Square® Crosscut 4-Patch or 9-Patch Ruler with the edges of your fabric will show you if your strips and seams are accurate, leading to perfect sections for a 4- or 9-patch block.

Review the following pages for instructions on how to use each of the Square in a Square® rulers or visit our website at **squareinasquare.com** for instructional videos.

Remember, all our rulers remove the "human element," which set you up for success with all your patchwork.

Sewing Machine
Use a clean, well-oiled machine with a size 70 or 80 needle. Make sure the tension is adjusted to produce a smooth seam. Many beginners become frustrated with piecing because of their machines, not their skill level.

Iron
A heavy, hot steam iron will improve the quality of your work. Keep it close to your machine for frequent pressing. Always press towards the darker area or the area without seams. More damage is done during the pressing stage than any other. Do not overwork your fabric.

Batting
There are many choices in batting. A poly/cotton blend seems to give the best results and gives the quilt an antique look. Pretreat the batting according to the instructions on the packaging or simply open the package and sandwich the quilt.

Fabric Dye
For an antique look, dye your quilt once completed. Dilute a box of ecru or tan fabric dye in a cup of hot water. Set your washing machine to a delicate or short cycle with a warm wash and cool rinse. Once the tub is full, add the diluted dye and agitate for a few minutes to mix the dye and water. Add your quilt and remove immediately after the final rinse. Stretch out and lay flat to dry or pop it in the dryer. There are many products on the market that age your fabric. Research carefully and beware.

Order Square in a Square® products online at squareinasquare.com.

Techniques

Square in a Square®
The Square in a Square® system consists of sewing strips and squares together to create squares within squares. When you sew first and then cut triangles, you will get much cleaner cuts and more accurate blocks or units for blocks. No more worrying about bias cuts and triangle stretch. You may cut straight or bias fabric strips. Never worry about having to cut or sew another triangle! You will be amazed at how versatile this technique can be. You will never again worry over triangle units.

Cutting
You can cut your strips of fabric from either yardage or fat quarters. Cutting instructions are given for full widths, 42"–44". If you are using fat quarters, simply cut twice as many strips as required for the pattern. You can cut about six layers of fabric at once by folding or layering the fabric. Make a clean-up cut on one edge. More than six layers may cause the fabric to shift, causing uneven cuts.

Machine Piecing
Machine piecing is strong, fast, and accurate. Learning to sew a scant ¼" seam is a must. Practice by stitching together three 1 ½" x 6" strips and press with seams out. If your seam allowance is accurate, the unit should measure 3 ½" x 6". Continue practicing this technique until you have perfected stitching a scant ¼" seam.

For more accurate piecing, try using spray starch on your fabrics before sewing. This is extremely helpful with miniatures or with pre-washed fabrics.

When you have two pieces that should fit together but don't, you will have to ease them together. Pin them well or use a stiletto and make them fit so seams and points match up. The fullest piece should feed through the machine on the bottom. The feed dogs will help ease the fullness more evenly, and the presser foot will slightly ease the top layer.

Chain Piecing
Chain piecing has always been a natural for me. I did it before I knew someone else had invented it! You can keep sewing units, one after another, without lifting the presser foot or stopping to cut threads. When it's time to move on to another part of the pattern, or you have about a mile of pieces on the back of your machine, you can stop and cut them apart.

I also use a runner, which is a small scrap of fabric that I run into the machine when I don't have a pattern piece to sew, or if I need to stop chain piecing. It leaves the machine in neutral and ready to sew the next chain. By using a runner and the chain piecing method, you won't have a mess with clipping hundreds of loose threads or lifting the presser foot every few seconds. There are so many reasons for doing this. I implore you to learn this.

Appliqué
There are numerous appliqué techniques for creating your designs. Appliqué designs can be simple or extremely intricate and can be stitched by hand or machine. I prefer a template-free method with a needle-turn appliqué stitch. Try them all and practice to master your favorite.

QUICK TIP

I never cut a whole quilt top out at the same time for multiple reasons:
- *It gets boring*
- *I don't want to stand at the table that long*
- *I can't change my mind and be creative*
- *If I never get back to it, I have cut/wasted fabric*
- *A dreaded PIG (see Definitions on page "PIGS" on page 51)*
- *What if I read or cut wrong*
- *I want to see "it" sewn together*
- *I want to make sure my fabric choices are "playing well" together*
- *I may want to change the size of quilt top*

FAQ

Why do you recommend not pre-washing my fabric?
I find piecing is more accurate with the sizing left in the fabric. If I'm concerned about colors running, I test a small piece of fabric and treat as necessary. I also like the sunscreen left in it during storage. It keeps the fabric fresh until I'm ready to use it. I also like the cotton batting and cotton fabric to shrink together after the quilt is finished. It gives it the antique look and feel I love so much!

What do I do with the fabric trimmed off the basic square?
Use that funny triangle piece to sew to the side of a smaller center square. You don't always have to use freshly-cut pieces of fabric. You can use waste or scraps from any previous option cutting, as long as the piece is large enough to get a good trim on your Square in a Square® option. That is how most of my smaller or miniature quilts are made.

Why do some Options trim up to the point of the center square and others leave ¼" on the tip of the center square?
This moves the seam allowances so that when you cut the option apart, the points of the triangles won't be lost in your next seam. Different options need the seam allowance in different places.

Can I round up the size of my cuts?
When cutting strips it may be easier to cut ¼" than ⅛". You can always round the strip size up to the nearest ¼" because the excess will be trimmed off.

What presser foot do you recommend for sewing options together?
I highly recommend a ¼" inch foot without a flange. This will help achieve the scant ¼" seam without relying on the ¼" mark on the machine itself.

How do I keep my points sharp?
Use a stiletto at the junctions of your seams to hold your squares in place while sewing. This works better than a pin. When a pin is pushed down and back through the fabric where multiple seams are located, it can move the exact point of your triangle and cause your piece to be off when you open to press. A stiletto can keep seam allowance flaps in place and keep points sharper. Remember that the right tool for the job gives us better work and makes the job easier.

What about the bias edge?
This is the one question I get asked most often. When you are sewing strips and squares for the basic square, you are working with the straight grain. This helps keep your units more stable. All of the cutting, sewing and pressing in the Square in a Square® system is on the straight grain to help keep your work flat and your points sharp. Once you trim the basic square for whatever option you choose, your block will then have a bias edge. You can continue to add to your block or use the option as a block by itself. As you connect your blocks, you will again be working with the straight grain. All of the steps that normally stretch your work are taken care of in building a basic square along the straight grain. If you are having trouble with a bias edge, place it on the bottom next to the feed dogs to help feed it into your machine when sewing two units together.

Do you have any additional tips or recommended reading?
Spray starch can be a quilter's best friend! Use on large units or pre-washed fabrics for stability. I highly recommend several books by Harriet Hargrave. For more information about quilting fabric, read *From Fiber to Fabric: The Essential Guide to Quiltmaking Textiles* or check out *Heirloom Machine Quilting: A Comprehensive Guide to Hand-Quilting Effects Using Your Sewing Machine* for tips and tricks on machine quilting like a pro.

Finishing

Squaring Up Blocks

Before assembling your quilt you will want to check each block to make sure that all the corners are square. Lay each block out on a smooth, flat surface and use an acrylic ruler on top of the block to see if your corners are 90° square. Trim as little as necessary. Also, make sure they are all the same size and that you have a ¼" seam allowance on all edges.

Straight Setting

Setting refers to the arrangement of the blocks of your quilt. Blocks can be straight set, alternating blocks with plain squares or other blocks, in any pattern you wish. Whether you choose to set your quilt straight or on point, you can separate rows with sashing and/or setting squares.

Sew blocks in rows, alternating setting squares or other blocks, then sew rows together.

Sew blocks in rows, along with sashing strips, then sew rows together.

Sew blocks in rows, along with sashing strips and setting squares, then sew rows together.

Diagonal Setting

There are many variations on how to piece a quilt together. One setting method is to set blocks diagonally, or on point. This technique will generally make the block, and overall quilt, look more intricate. Even the simplest blocks can have more pizzazz by setting them on an angle. When a quilt is set on point, you will sew your rows of blocks diagonally, finishing each end with either side setting triangles or corner triangles.

Side setting triangles are created by cutting squares diagonally, as shown, to yield four half square triangles. Corner triangles are created by cutting a square in half diagonally, yielding two triangle units.

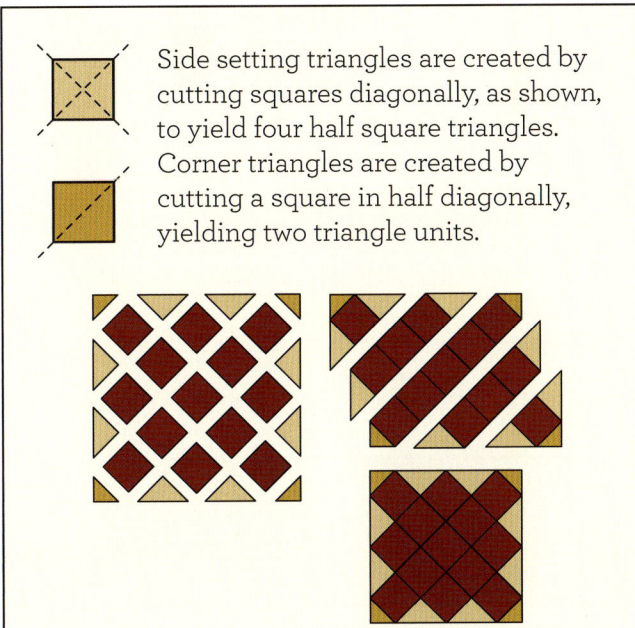

Sewn (finished) Size of Block	Cut Square for Side Setting Triangles	Cut Square for Corner Triangles
2	4 ⅛	2 ⅜
3	5 ½	3
4	7	3 ¾
5	8 ⅜	4 ½
6	9 ¾	5 ⅛
7	11 ¼	5 ⅞
8	12 ⅝	6 ⅝
9	14	7 ¼
10	15 ½	8
12	18 ¼	9 ⅜

Borders

Adding a border to your quilt will help frame in and highlight your quilt design. To find the length for your quilt border, measure the quilt from raw edge to raw edge through the middle. Cut and sew two strips of fabric along the length of your quilt. Repeat for the width. Measuring along the outside edges can cause the border to ripple. You may have to ease the border to fit. If so, place the fullness on the bottom against the feed dogs.

Batting and Backing

For the best look, choose fabric with a design rather than a solid color for your backing. Cut both the batting and backing at least 4" larger than the quilt top. Layer the quilt top, batting, and backing together and baste.

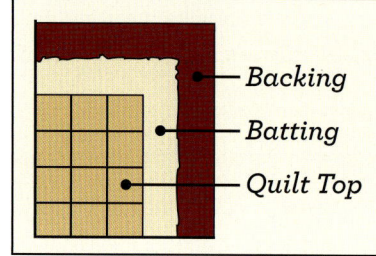

Backing
Batting
Quilt Top

Hand Quilting

Hand quilting is a fun, although time-consuming, technique, but can add lots of character to your quilt. Heavy quilting is always admired. Be sure to spend time planning your quilting to enhance the design. Make your stitches as small and even as you can.

Machine Quilting

Machine quilting has greatly improved over the years and can also produce great results. Small and medium quilts are the easiest to maneuver. A walking foot is a must-have for straight line quilting and binding. By dropping the feed dogs and using a darning foot, you will be able to free motion any design. Use cotton thread in the bobbin and nylon .004 on the top, adjusting the tension as necessary. Research the type of thread that you want to use. Thread color, weight and fiber type will have a lot to do with the finished look of your quilt. This is an important detail, often overlooked.

Squaring Up the Quilt

After quilting, trim the backing and batting even with the quilt top edges. It is likely that your corners and edges may have become slightly uneven. Lay your quilt out on a smooth, flat surface and use a ruler or t-square to see if your corners are square. Trim as little as necessary to achieve 90° corners. Next, fold the short ends of your quilt towards the middle. If your edges are off by 1" or less, you have done well and will want to leave your quilt as is. If the edges are off by more than 1", trim the edges until they are equal. Be careful not to get too carried away with squaring up your quilt or you may throw off the balance of your border and the overall look of your quilt.

QUICK TIP

- learn and regularly practice a "scant" seam allowance.

QUICK TIP *saving fabric:*

- surround strips for Options that trim up to the tip can be cut to the exact length of the center square—it will look too short, but when trimmed it will be perfect!
- cut large pieces first and work down to the smallest—small cuts can always be cut from the fabric left over from larger cuts

QUICK TIP

- Use spray starch on washed fabric only if you must. **Never** wet blocks as you iron, especially if you are proud of the way they look and fit. More units are ruined at the iron than anywhere else.

QUICK TIP *surround strips:*

- you may notice that a surround strip width may be slightly different in a pattern versus the charts—this is to keep the cutting of the quilt simple

First Things First

The center diamond and diamond options are really very simple. There are only a few things you need to know to complete any of these incredible designs. Make sure you understand these points before getting started. Remember, the DVD and our website have great visual instructions on Options #1–#20. Everything you need to know is included in the two locations. Also, remember you can always call or email us anytime. We are here to teach you along the way or can point you towards one of our many certified instructors out there. Check the website for one near you.

1. Know how to cut accurate strips and squares.
2. Sew a scant ¼" seam allowance and press neatly.
3. Know how to trim the basic building options of the square – Options #1, #3 and #4.
4. Know how to cut the diamond unit from a strip. Keep telling yourself "it is just like a square." Which means, if I cut a 3" strip, I also cross cut at 3".
5. Know how to trim the basic building options of the diamond – Options #7, #18, #19 and #20. All of the diamond options trim from one of these beginning cuts. Remember: if you are cutting through the option at a point, you must move or slide the Square in a Square® ruler over to a new point or line of reference on the tool. Study these basic squares and basic diamond units before you start a quilt. When you get frustrated, try using "square" logic or just email or call us. We are here to help you along the way.
6. When you select a quilt design, look for the required option and study it at the front of the book. The pattern gives you the center cut square or diamond and strip sizes for the design you have chosen. You must look at both the option at the front and the quilt design as you work on your masterpiece.
7. It is a good idea to make sure you understand the process before you begin cutting and sewing on your chosen fabric. Making a few samples is always a good idea. After you have read through the instructions, it is time to sew. Actually going through the steps will help you understand. Hands-on and doing it really brings it all together.
8. After you have sewn around the diamond center and made the first cut, it becomes a rectangle unit. We then refer to the short sides as the top or bottom, north or south. The long sides are the east and west of the rectangle unit. In some patterns the correct color location is important. Also, the short sides are a smaller width of strip – these are all row 2 surround strips.
9. The Square in a Square Reference Book is the core workbook for the Square in a Square® system. This technique does build on each step. We did not print duplicate information unless it was vital to the diamond process. How to figure fabric for the options and pattern adapting steps as well as the options that pertain to the square centers are only in the Square in a Square Reference Book. These two books are the core workbooks for the technique or system and should be used together.

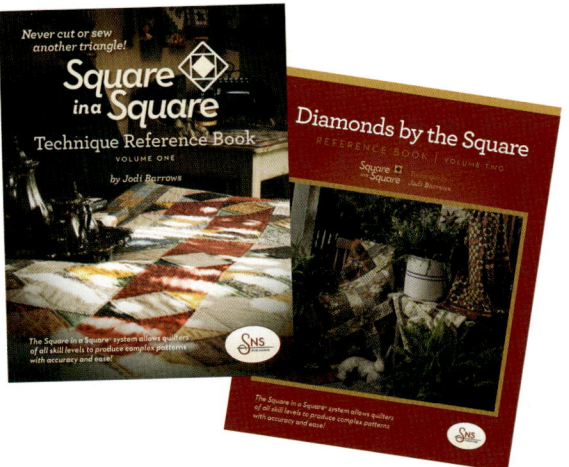

Ruler Instructions

Cross-Cut 4-Patch Ruler

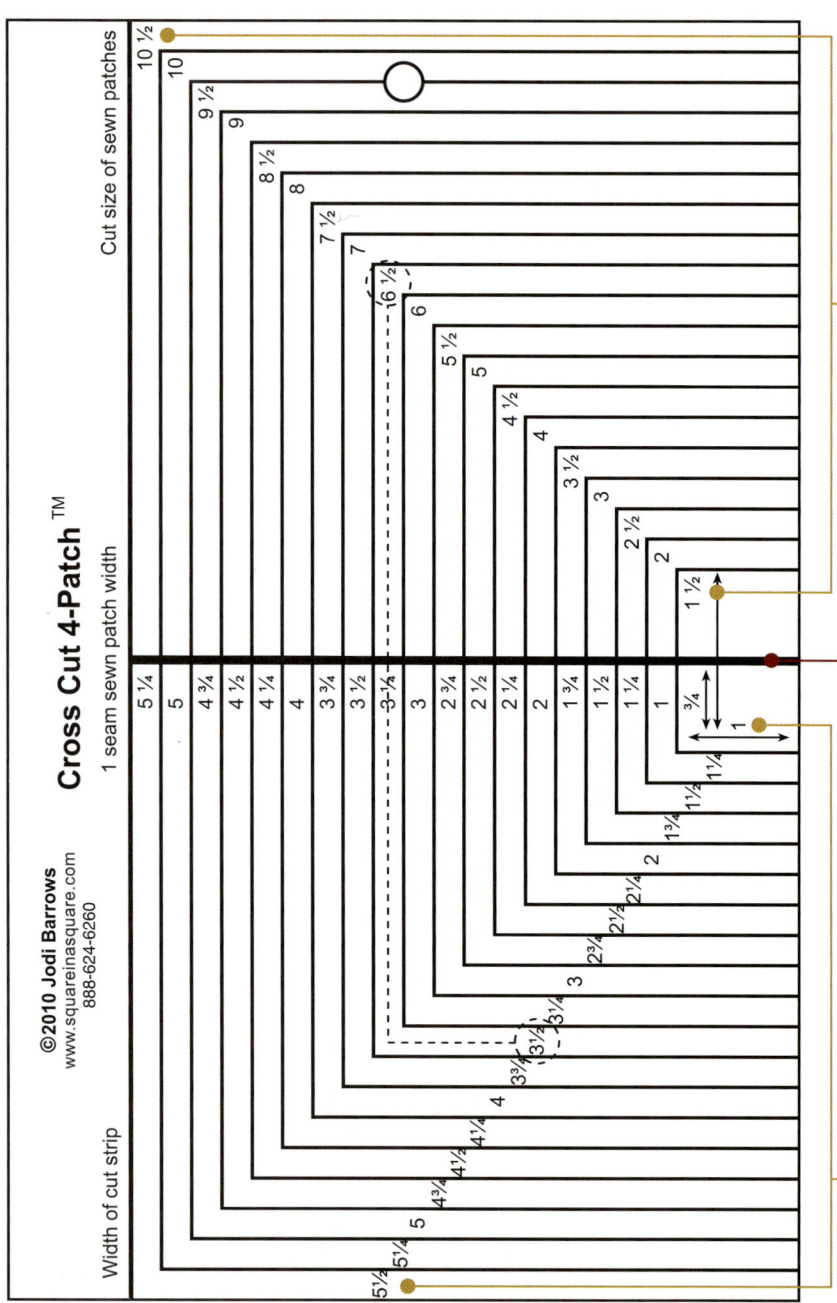

Align your sewn strips along this side of the ruler to cut.

This set of numbers (1 ½"–10 ½") is equal to the unfinished size of your patches.

Line up the center seam of your sewn strips with this thick line. This set of numbers (¾"–5 ¼") should be equal to the width of one sewn (finished) strip and one raw edge.

Use both of these sets of numbers to quickly find the cut size of strips needed for any sewn size 4-patch unit. Find the measurement on the top/right for your finished patch size and follow the line to the bottom/left. This is the strip width needed for this size of unit.

This set of numbers (1"–5 ½") should be equal to the width of your cut strips or squares.

Cross-Cut 9-Patch Ruler

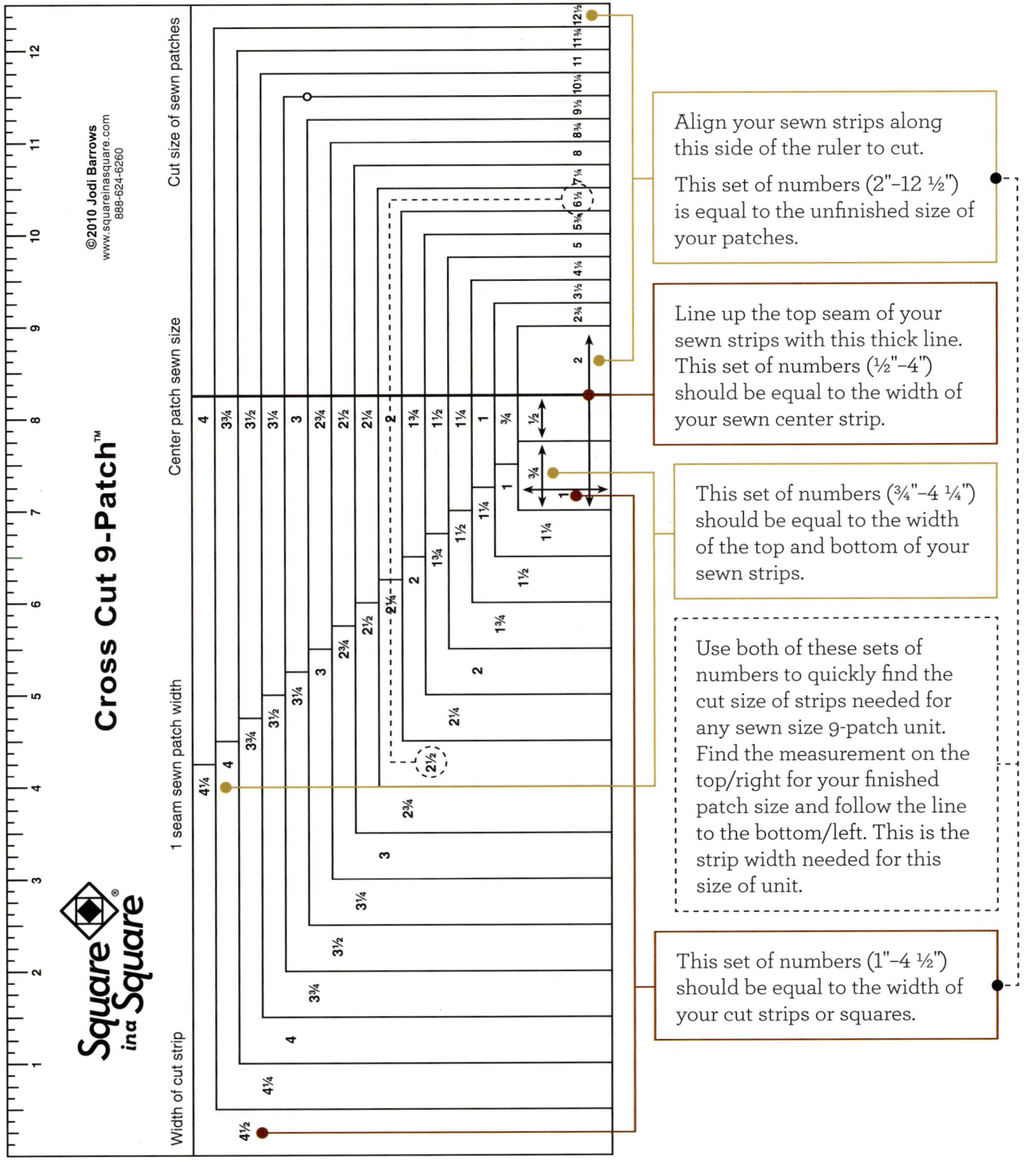

How to use the Cross-Cut 4-Patch Ruler

Sew two equal width strips of fabric along the length of the strips, then press with the seams to the dark. Place the 4-Patch Ruler on your sewn strips, lining up the seam with the thick line on the middle of the ruler and clean-cut the ends.

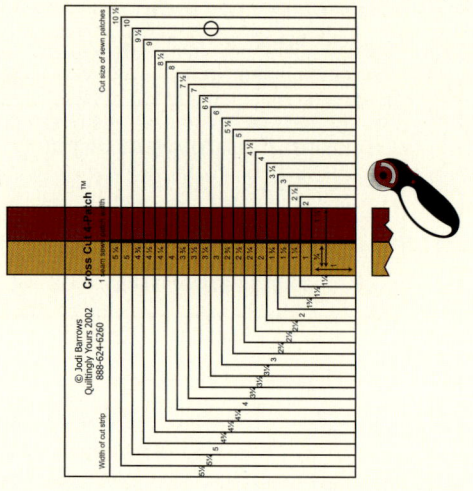

Line up your seam with the thick line on the middle of the ruler. The measurements along this line should equal half of the width of your sewn strips. Align your clean-cut edge with the desired finished size indicated by the measurements along the top or right side of the ruler and crosscut along the edge with a rotary cutter. The measurements along the bottom or left side of the ruler indicate the finished width of your section.

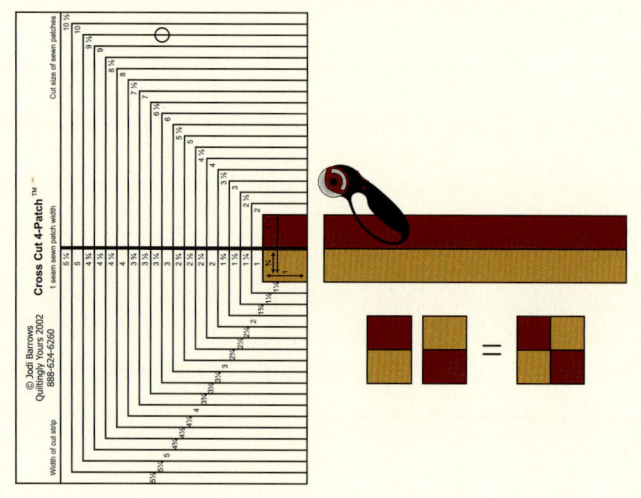

How to use the Cross-Cut 9-Patch Ruler

Sew three equal width strips of fabric along the length of the strips, then press with the seams to the dark. Place the 9-Patch Ruler on your sewn strips, lining up the top seam with the thick line on the middle of the ruler and clean-cut the ends.

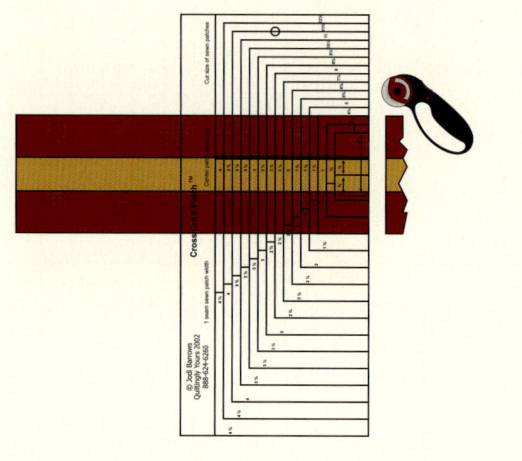

Line up the top seam with the thick line on the middle of the ruler. The measurements along the thick line should equal the width of your center strip. Align your clean-cut edge with the desired finished size indicated by the measurements along the top or right side of the ruler and crosscut along the edge of the ruler with a rotary cutter. The measurements along the farthest left side or bottom of the ruler indicate the finished width of your section. The second set of measurements on the left indicate the width of the top and bottom strips of your section.

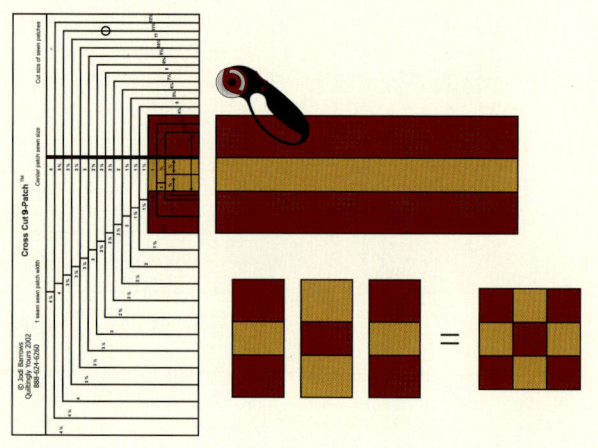

4- and 9-Patch Sizing

4-Patch
Instructions on pages 10 & 12.

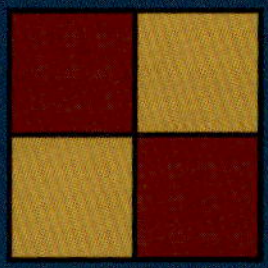

Sewn (finished) Size of Block	Sewn (finished) Size of Single Square	Cut Strip Size for Strata & Crosscut Size	Cut (unfinished) Size of Block
1	½	1	1 ½
1 ½	¾	1 ¼	2
2	1	1 ½	2 ½
2 ½	1 ¼	1 ¾	3
3	1 ½	2	3 ½
3 ½	1 ¾	2 ¼	4
4	2	2 ½	4 ½
4 ½	2 ¼	2 ¾	5
5	2 ½	3	5 ½
5 ½	2 ¾	3 ¼	6
6	3	3 ½	6 ½
6 ½	3 ¼	3 ¾	7
7	3 ½	4	7 ½
7 ½	3 ¾	4 ¼	8
8	4	4 ½	8 ½
8 ½	4 ¼	4 ¾	9
9	4 ½	5	9 ½
9 ½	4 ¾	5 ¼	10
10	5	5 ½	10 ½

9-Patch
Instructions on pages 11 & 12.

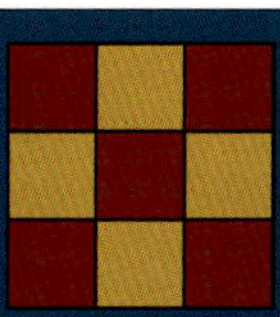

Sewn (finished) Size of Block	Sewn (finished) Size of Single Square	Cut Strip Size for Strata & Crosscut Size	Cut (unfinished) Size of Block
1 ½	½	1	2
2 ¼	¾	1 ¼	2 ¾
3	1	1 ½	3 ½
3 ¾	1 ¼	1 ¾	4 ¼
4 ½	1 ½	2	5
5 ¼	1 ¾	2 ¼	5 ¾
6	2	2 ½	6 ½
6 ¾	2 ¼	2 ¾	7 ¼
7 ½	2 ½	3	8
8 ¼	2 ¾	3 ¼	8 ¾
9	3	3 ½	9 ½
9 ¾	3 ¼	3 ¾	10 ¼
10 ½	3 ½	4	11
11 ¼	3 ¾	4 ¼	11 ¾
12	4	4 ½	12 ½

QUICK TIP
- the size of your Option is determined by three things: center square, seam allowance and proper trimming of the Option; pay attention to the way you lay the ruler on the fabric pieces.

QUICK TIP
- a strip of fabric is an average of 40", cut selvedge to selvedge, from yard goods
- when rounding numbers, always round up
- remember to sew only a scant ¼" seam
- spray starch can help keep washed fabric from moving while cutting and sewing

R-5 Mini Ruler

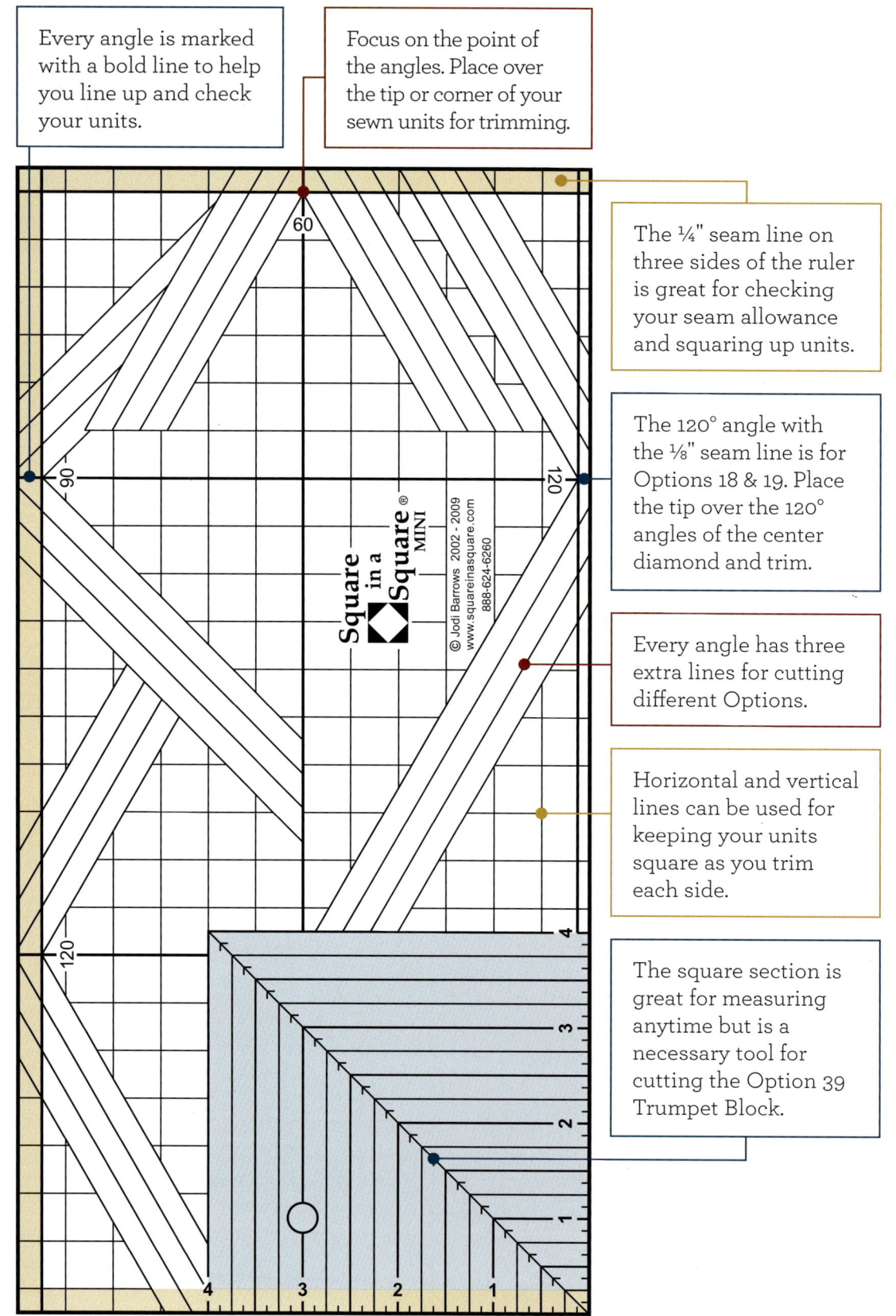

Every angle is marked with a bold line to help you line up and check your units.

Focus on the point of the angles. Place over the tip or corner of your sewn units for trimming.

The ¼" seam line on three sides of the ruler is great for checking your seam allowance and squaring up units.

The 120° angle with the ⅛" seam line is for Options 18 & 19. Place the tip over the 120° angles of the center diamond and trim.

Every angle has three extra lines for cutting different Options.

Horizontal and vertical lines can be used for keeping your units square as you trim each side.

The square section is great for measuring anytime but is a necessary tool for cutting the Option 39 Trumpet Block.

R-8 Original Ruler

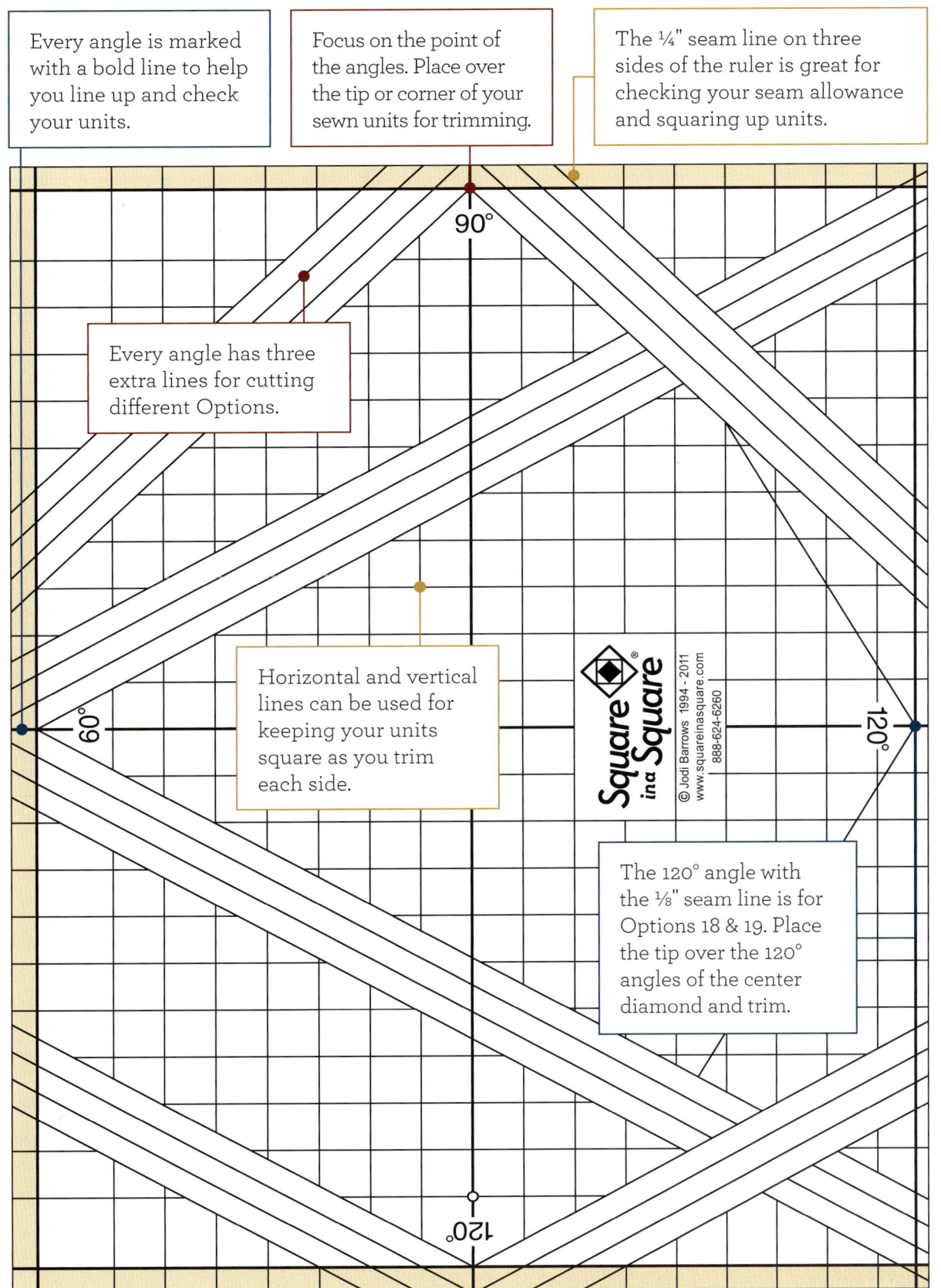

Every angle is marked with a bold line to help you line up and check your units.

Focus on the point of the angles. Place over the tip or corner of your sewn units for trimming.

The ¼" seam line on three sides of the ruler is great for checking your seam allowance and squaring up units.

Every angle has three extra lines for cutting different Options.

Horizontal and vertical lines can be used for keeping your units square as you trim each side.

The 120° angle with the ⅛" seam line is for Options 18 & 19. Place the tip over the 120° angles of the center diamond and trim.

Basic Square—Option 1

The basic square will be the foundation for most of the options in the Square in a Square® system.

① Lay a surround strip face up on your sewing machine. Place the first center square face down on the strip, lining up the edges. Sew a scant ¼" along the edge of the square. Lay the next square down on the strip (only a small space between squares is needed) and continue on in a chain piecing method. Repeat for the opposite side of the square. Do not open either piece of fabric when you sew.

② Cut the squares apart, then press open—seams out.

③ Sew short strips to the other two sides of the square and press open—seams out.

④ Cutting an Option 1 is easy using the Square in a Square® ruler. Match any corner of the center square with the 90° angle on the ruler. Trim, leaving a ¼" seam allowance on all four sides. You may notice that the corners are sometimes blunted just a little, but this won't affect the finished square at all.

⑤ You now have an Option 1.

MAGIC MATH
determine strip width by measuring the cut center square, divide that measurement in half and add ¼"; refer to the sizing chart on page 50.

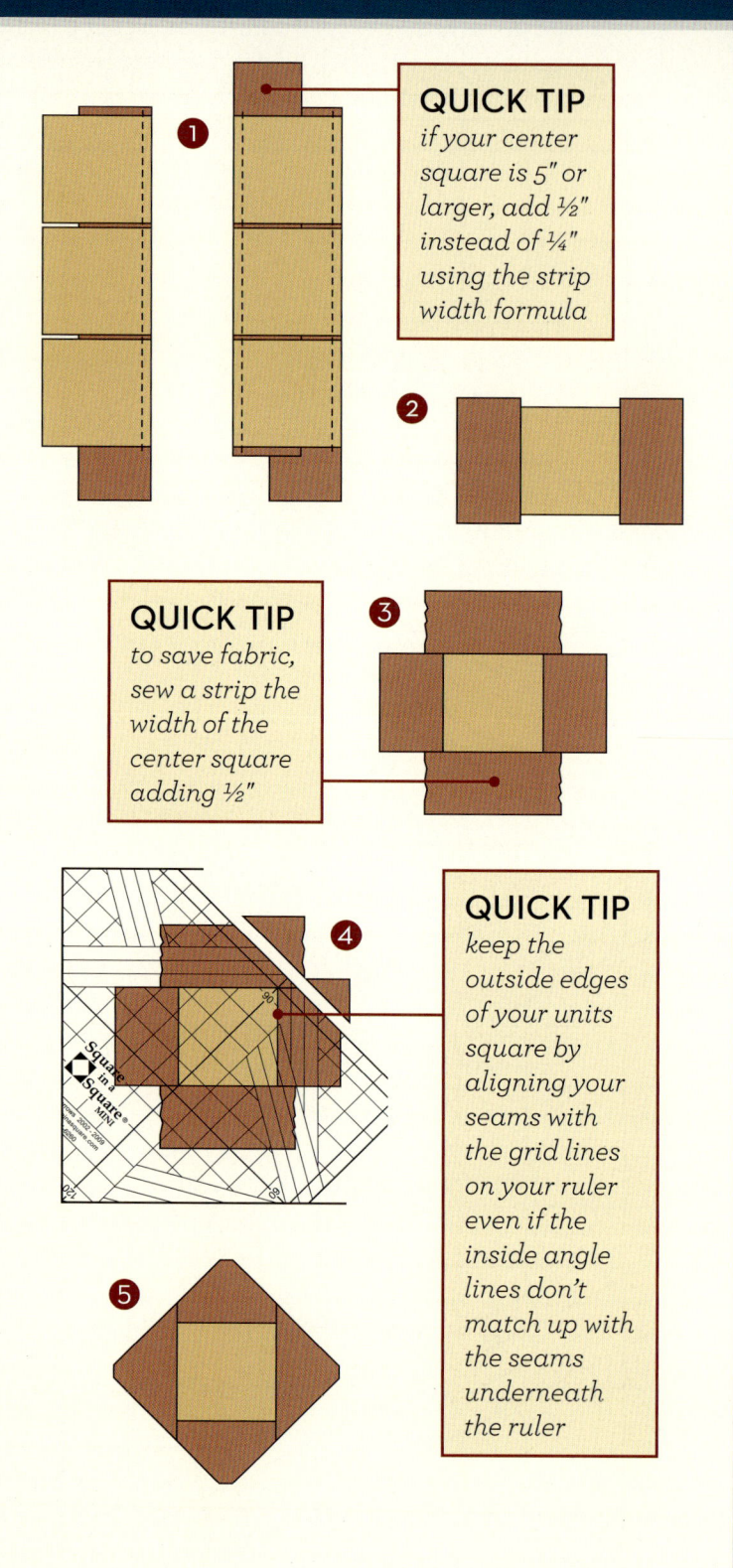

QUICK TIP
if your center square is 5" or larger, add ½" instead of ¼" using the strip width formula

QUICK TIP
to save fabric, sew a strip the width of the center square adding ½"

QUICK TIP
keep the outside edges of your units square by aligning your seams with the grid lines on your ruler even if the inside angle lines don't match up with the seams underneath the ruler

Option 2—Expanding the Basic Square

You can expand the size of a basic square by continuing to add strips in the same method. Keep adding rounds until the square is the size needed.

1. Sew a basic square and trim as you would an Option 1.
2. Sew a second row of surround strips to your square.
3. Match any corner of the new center square with the corresponding angle on the ruler. Trim all four corners as you would an Option 1, leaving a ¼" seam allowance.
4. You can continue adding surround strips until your block is the desired size. You now have an Option 2.

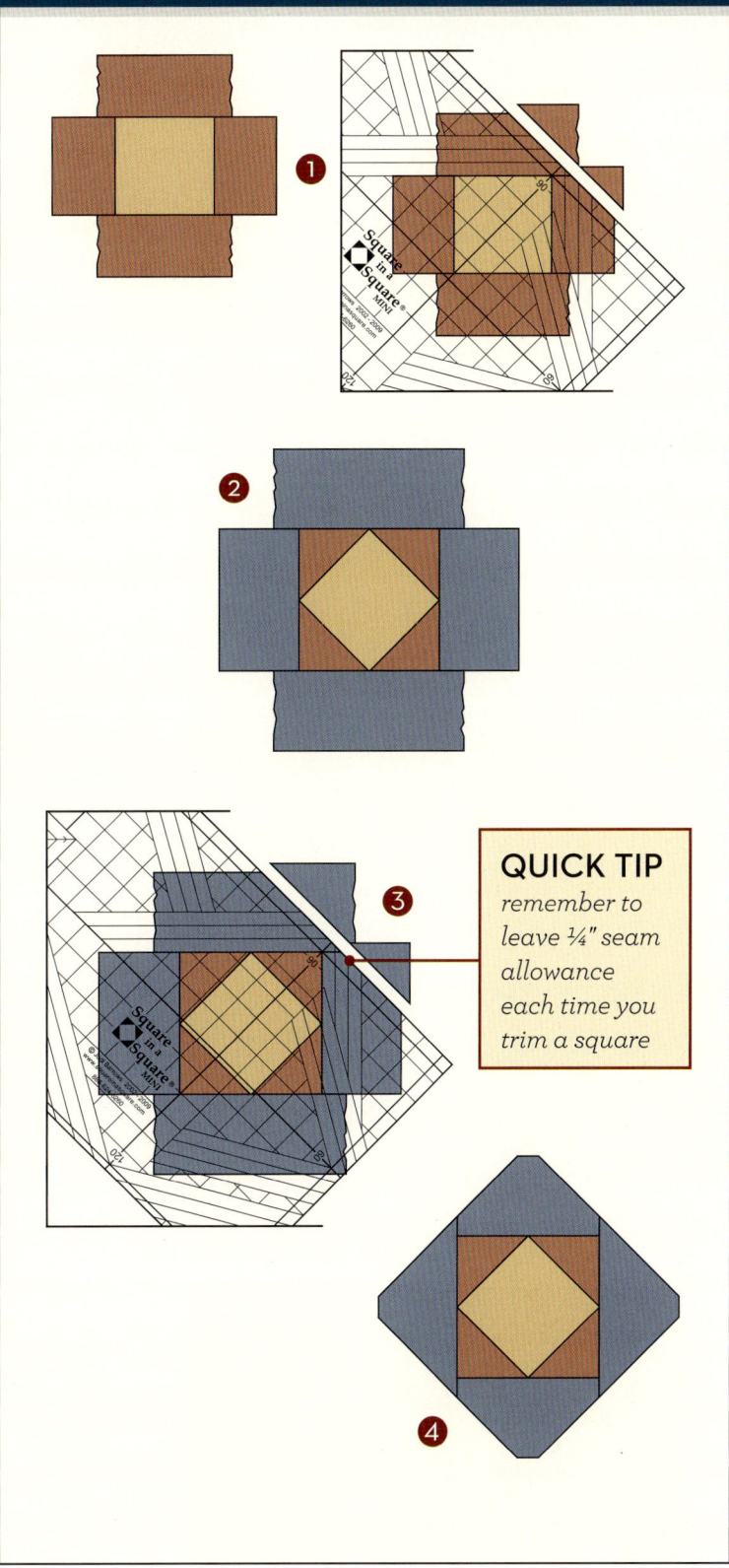

QUICK TIP
remember to leave ¼" seam allowance each time you trim a square

MAGIC MATH
determine strip width by measuring the cut center square, divide that measurement in half and add ¼"; re-measure your cut square each time you add surround strips (add ½" instead of ¼" if your square is 5" or larger); refer to the sizing chart on page 50.

Option 3—Flying Geese

1. Sew a basic square. Trim opposing corners as you would an Option 1, leaving a ¼" seam allowance.
2. Trim the remaining corners up to the point of the center square.
3. Cut in half from tip to tip as shown.
4. You now have an Option 3— Flying Geese.

MAGIC MATH
*determine the center square cut size by figuring what the **sewn** (finished) measurement of the triangle section should be and add ⅞"; refer to the sizing chart on page 50.*

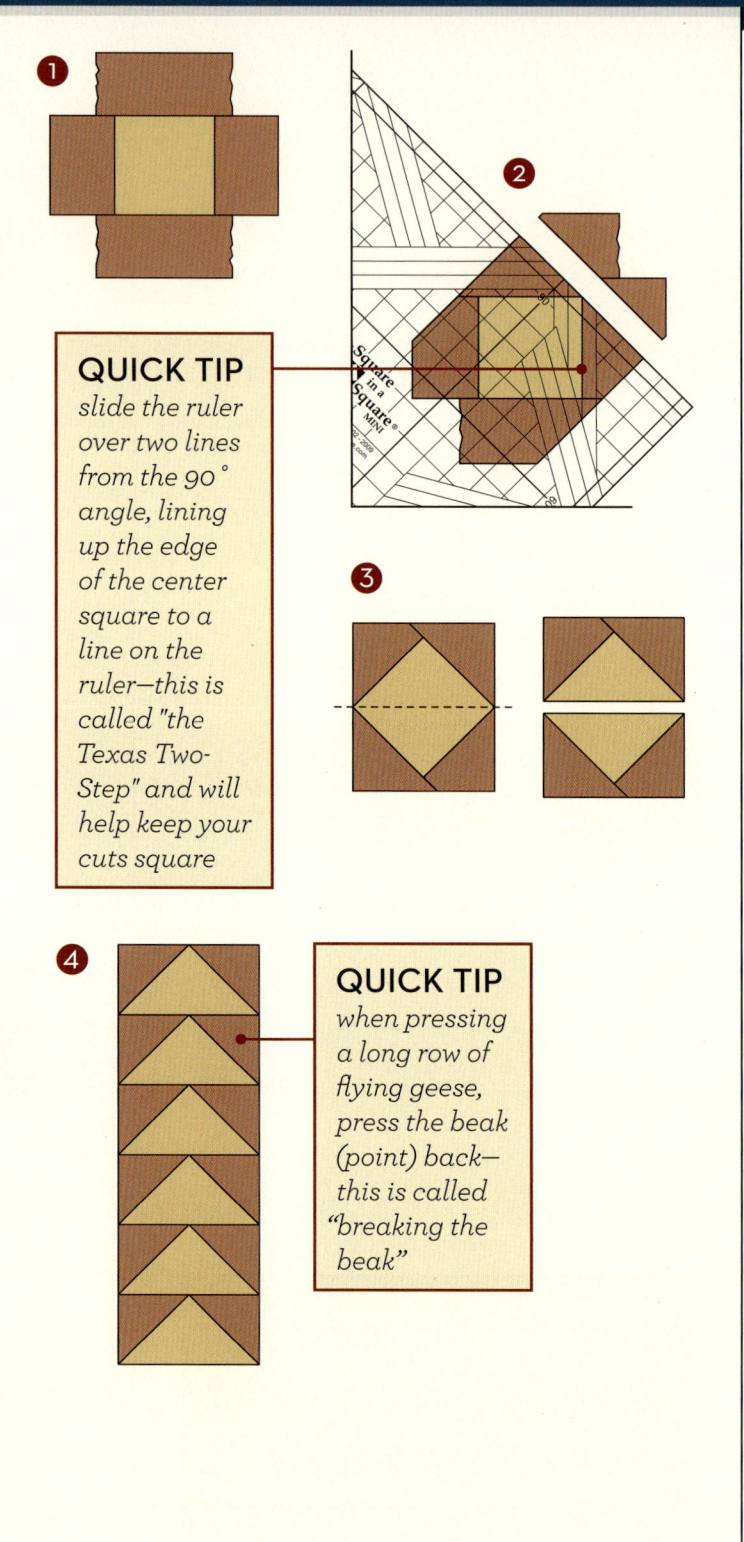

QUICK TIP
slide the ruler over two lines from the 90° angle, lining up the edge of the center square to a line on the ruler—this is called "the Texas Two-Step" and will help keep your cuts square

QUICK TIP
when pressing a long row of flying geese, press the beak (point) back— this is called "breaking the beak"

Option 4—Half Square Triangles

You can make four half square triangle squares by cutting this option into fourths.

1. Sew a basic square.
2. Trim all four corners up to the point of the center square.
3. Cut in half from tip to tip as shown to get four half square triangles.
4. You now have an Option 4—Half Square Triangles.

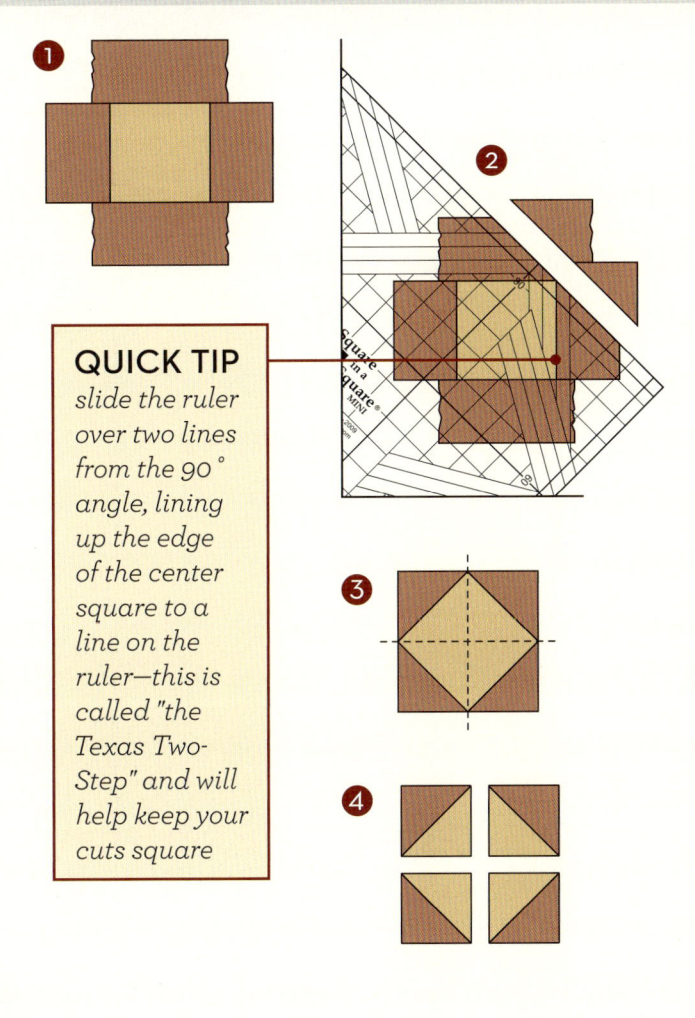

QUICK TIP
slide the ruler over two lines from the 90° angle, lining up the edge of the center square to a line on the ruler—this is called "the Texas Two-Step" and will help keep your cuts square

MAGIC MATH
determine desired half square triangle cut size, multiply by 1.414 and add ½" (round up to the nearest ⅛"); for example, if you want a 3" half square triangle (finished size 2 ½"), the formula would look like this: 3" × 1.414 + ½" = 4.742 or 4.75; refer to the sizing chart on page 50.

When figuring sizes for any quilt design, remember there are two sizes that you work with. The smaller size is the sewn (finished) or graph paper size. The larger size is the cut (unfinished) or raw size. Always make sure you are working with the correct size.

Basic Diamond—Option 7

You can use the Square in a Square® ruler to easily cut a diamond to use as the center of your block instead of a square.

① Cut a strip of fabric that will become your center diamond. Lay the Square in a Square® ruler on the strip, lining up a horizontal edge of the fabric with the 60° angle. Trim along the edge of the ruler.

② Rotate your fabric, lining up the edge with the 60° angle and cut the diamond segments the same length as the width of your strip. Check the angle every three to four cuts to make sure you are still cutting a 60° angle, recutting if necessary.

③ Cut and sew surround strips like a **Basic Square**, leaving a ¼" seam allowance. Do not open either piece of fabric when you sew.

④ Cut the diamonds apart, then press open—seams out.

⑤ Sew short strips to the other two sides of the diamond and press open—seams out. Use strips the width of the diamond plus ½" to save fabric. You now have a **Basic Diamond**.

⑥ Trim using the 60° angle on the short sides and the 120° angle on the long sides, leaving a ¼" seam allowance.

⑦ You now have an Option 7.

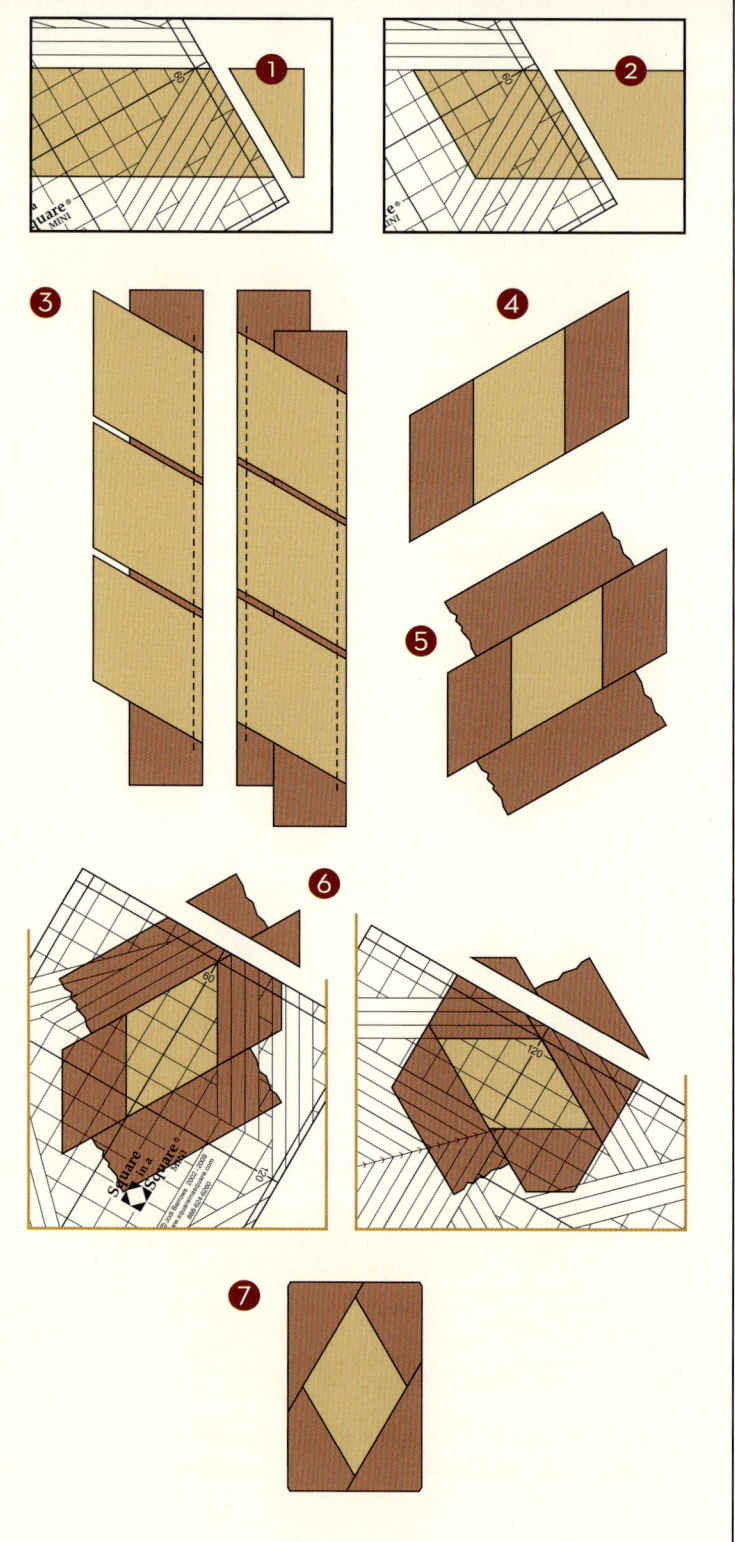

> **QUICK TIP**
> *step 4 can also look like a "z" if you cut them apart while the strips are folded together, either is correct*

Option 11

You can make larger corner square units by combining steps from Options 1, 2 and 4.

1. Sew a basic square and trim as you would an Option 1.
2. Add a second row of surround strips like an Option 2. Trim all four corners up to the point as you would an Option 4. Be careful not to cut too much or too little. The points should be sharp.
3. Cut in half horizontally and vertically from tip to tip of the square as shown.
4. You now have an Option 11.

> **QUICK TIP**
> trimming sequence is Option 1, Option 4

> **QUICK TIP**
> to resize any Option for your own designs, determine what size the center unit of your sewn (finished) Option needs to be; then look at the Option Sizing Charts on pages 50–66 for the correct cutting measurements

> **MAGIC MATH**
> determine desired corner square **sewn** (finished) size, multiply by 2 and add 1"

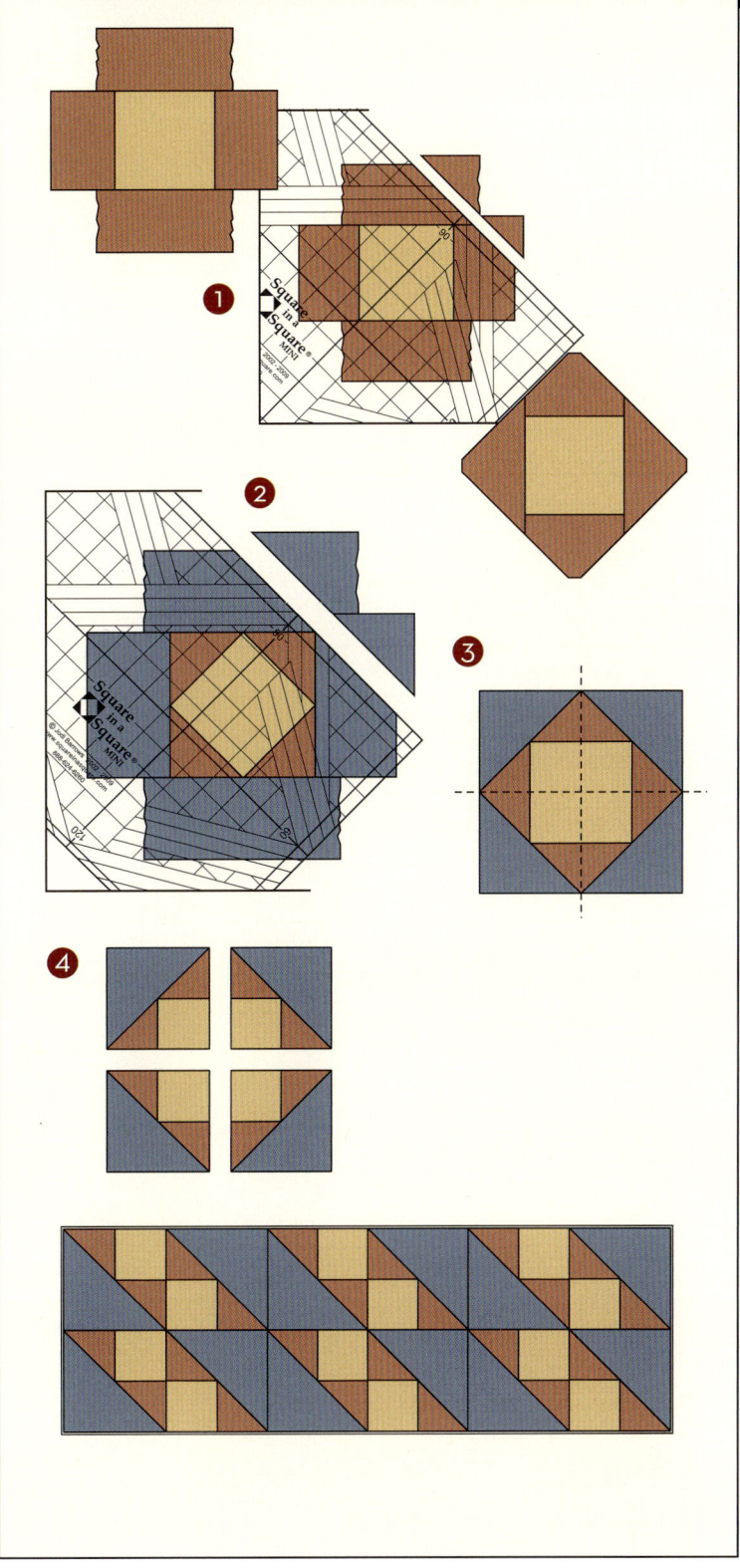

Option 14

1. Sew a basic square. Trim all four corners up to the point as you would an Option 4.
2. Add a second row of surround strips and trim as you would an Option 1, leaving a ¼" seam allowance.
3. Add a third row of surround strips and trim all four corners up to the point as you would an Option 4.
4. Cut in half horizontally and vertically from tip to tip of the square as shown.
5. You now have an Option 14.

> **QUICK TIP**
> *trimming sequence is Option 4, Option 1, Option 4*

> **QUICK TIP**
> *to resize any Option for your own designs, determine what size the center unit of your sewn (finished) Option needs to be; then look at the Option Sizing Charts on pages 50–66 for the correct cutting measurements*

> **MAGIC MATH**
> *determine desired half square triangle cut size, multiply by 1.414 and add ½" (round up to the nearest ⅛"); for example, if you want a 3" half square triangle (finished size 2 ½"), the formula would look like this:*
> *3" × 1.414 + ½" = 4.742 or 4.75*

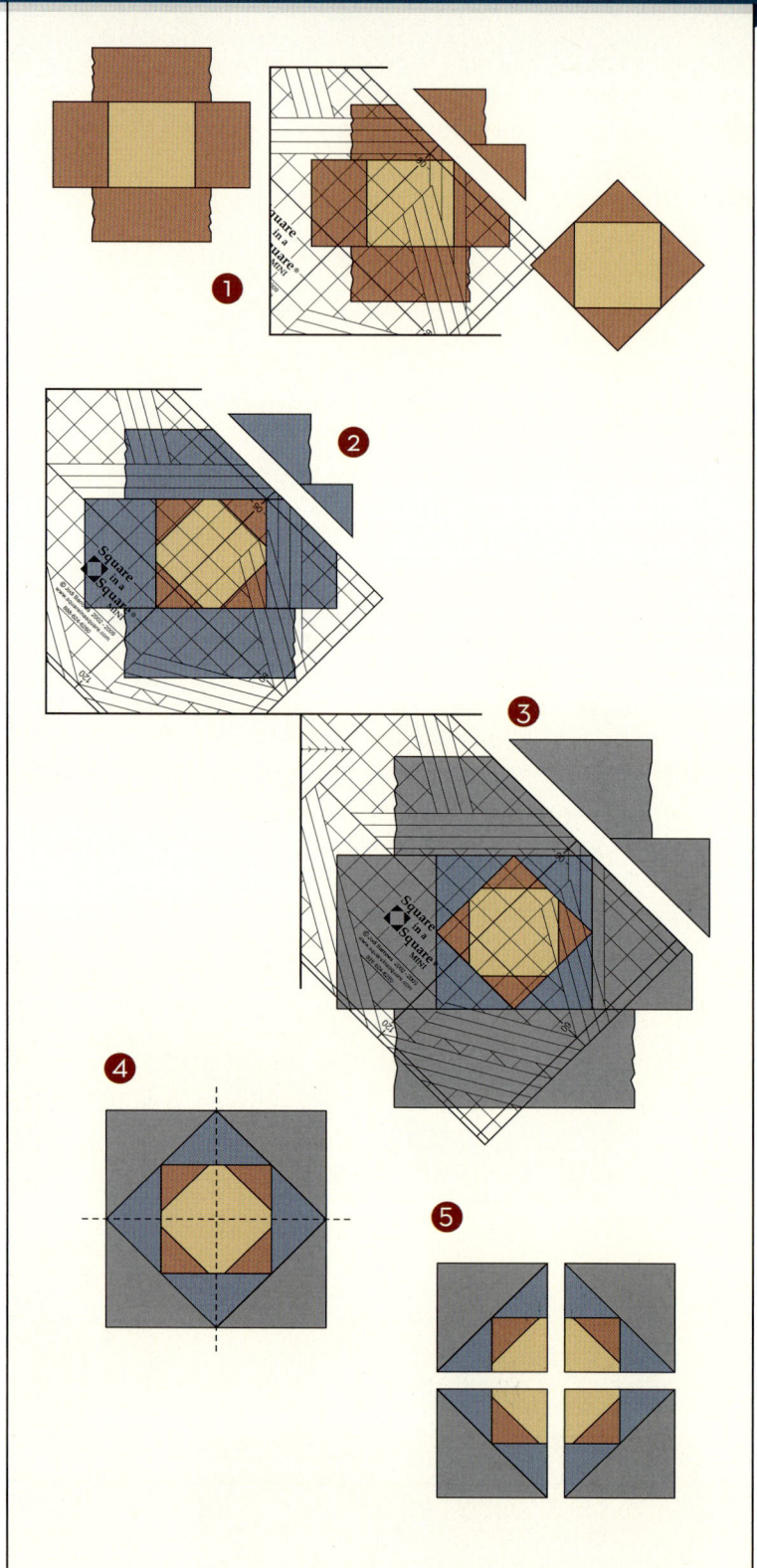

22

Option 18—Canadian Geese™

You can make Canadian Geese starting with a **Basic Diamond**.

1. Sew a **Basic Diamond**. Trim both 60° angles, leaving a ¼" seam allowance.
2. Trim the 120° angles, leaving only a ⅛" seam allowance. The difference in the seam allowances is necessary to move the points and seam allowance for sharp points on your finished block.
3. Cut in half horizontally through the sides of the center diamond, as shown.
4. You now have an Option 18.

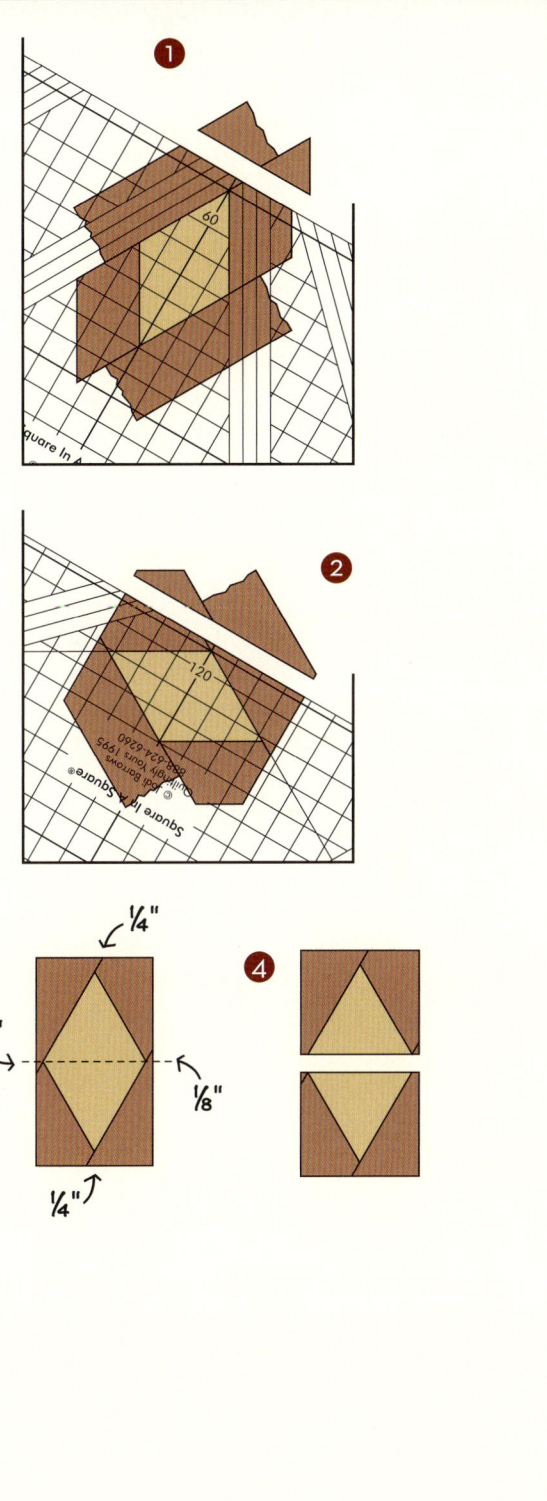

Option 19—Long Thin Triangle

1. Sew a **Basic Diamond**. Trim both 60° angles by dragging the 60° angle on the ruler down across a set of seams, one set of lines. After trimming this will leave a blunted edge on the diamond points. *Hint:* the blunted points should be a perfect ¼" opening.
2. Trim both 120° angles of the diamond by placing the 120° angle on the ruler with the ⅛" seam allowance at the point of the center diamond. This will leave ⅛" of fabric on the outside point of the diamond. This is necessary for acquiring the perfect point after the unit is cut and resewn.
3. Next cut the Option 19 in half top to bottom by using the 120° angle on the ruler with the ⅛" seam allowance. Place the ⅛" line at the fabric point of the diamond at the top and bottom. This will divide the ¼" opening into the perfect ⅛" that is required on each side of the point.
4. Use the edge of the ruler to cut horizontal perfectly through the 120° points of the diamond.
   Hint: the four option 19 units will have two sets of mirror image units. The two that match are kitty-corner of each other.

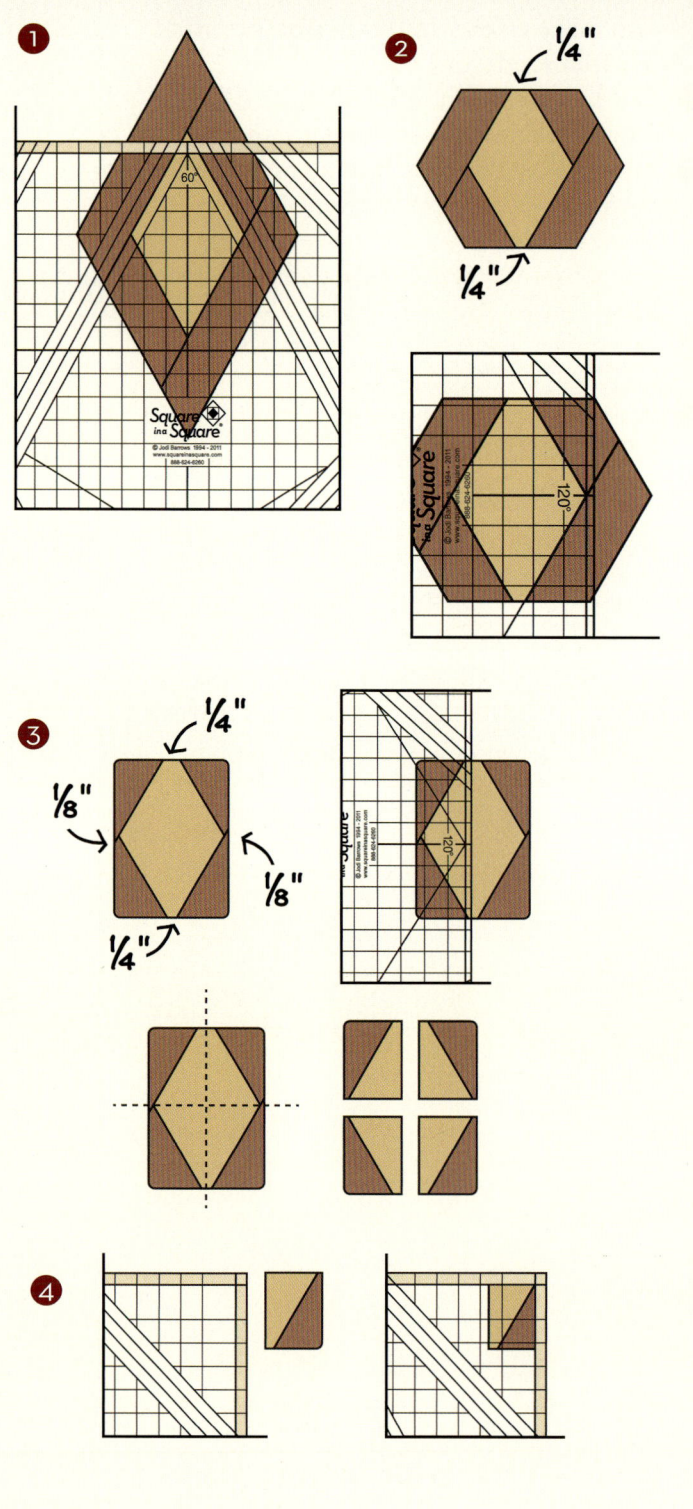

Option 20—Roof Top Triangles

1. Sew a **Basic Diamond**. To trim Option 20 place the diamond vertically. Trim both 60° angles, by dragging the 60° angle on the ruler down across the set of seams, one set of lines. After trimming this will leave a blunted edge across the top of the north and south points. This is necessary for acquiring the perfect point after the unit is cut and resewn.
   Hint: the blunt north and south should be a perfect ¼" opening.
2. Trim both 120° angles of the diamond by placing the 120° angle on the ruler with the ¼" seam allowance at the point of the center diamond. This will leave ¼" of fabric on the outside point of the diamond. Similar to the Option 7 diamond.
3. Next cut the Option 20 in half top to bottom by using the 120° angle on the ruler with the ⅛" seam allowance. Place the ⅛" line at the fabric point of the diamond at the top and bottom. This will divide the ¼" opening into the perfect ⅛" that is required on each side of the point.

Hint: Match the corner of the ruler to the corner of the Option 20 unit. The seam allowance can been seen or double-checked.

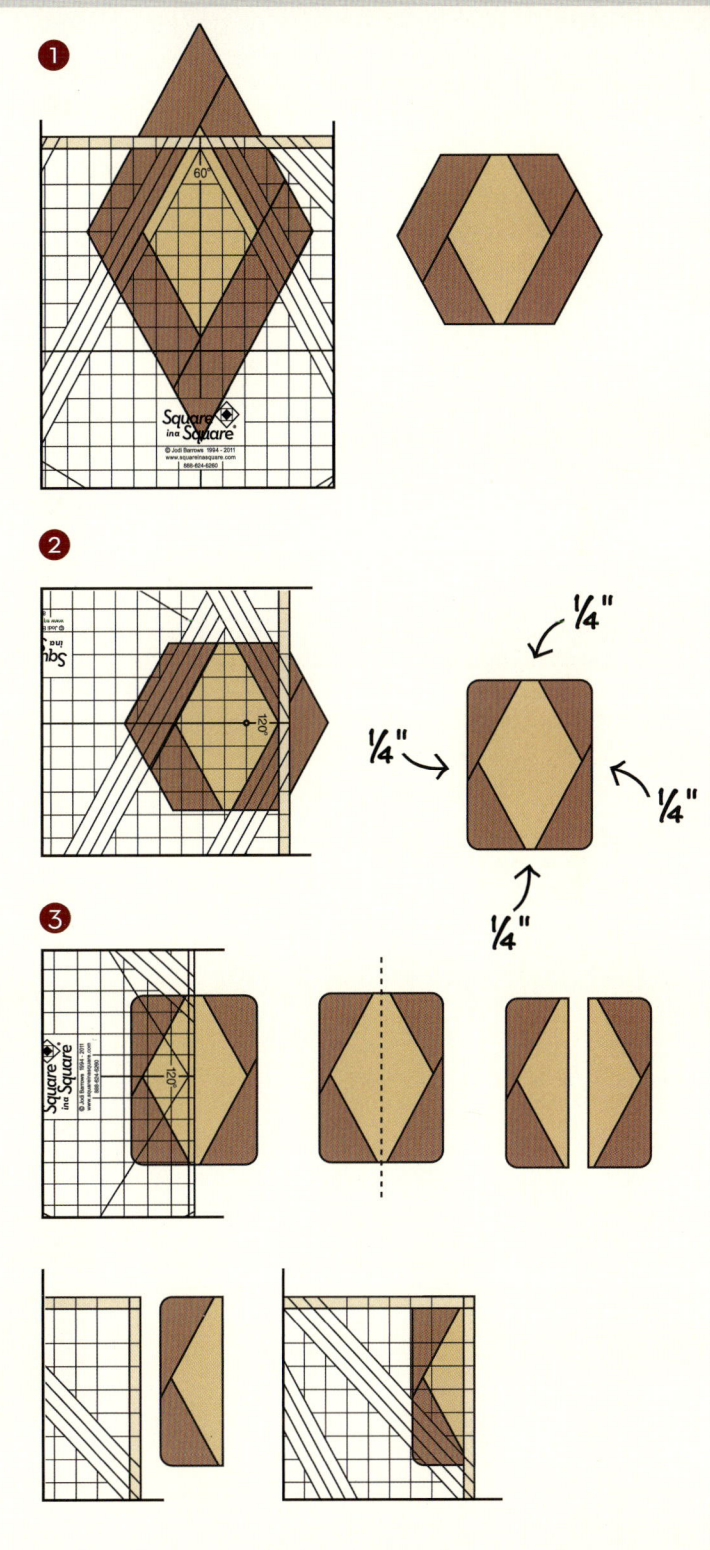

Option 21

Continue adding surround strips or rows until you have the size that is required.

① Sew a **Basic Diamond** and trim as you would an Option 7, leaving ¼" seam allowance on all four sides.

② Sew a second round of surround strips to your center rectangle.

③ Match any corner of the new rectangle with 90° angle on the ruler. Trim all four corners as you would an Option 1 leaving a ¼" seam allowance.

④ Continue adding surround strips or rows, always trimming with the 90° angle in the new corner of your square.

> **QUICK TIP**
> *trimming sequence is Option 7, Option 1*

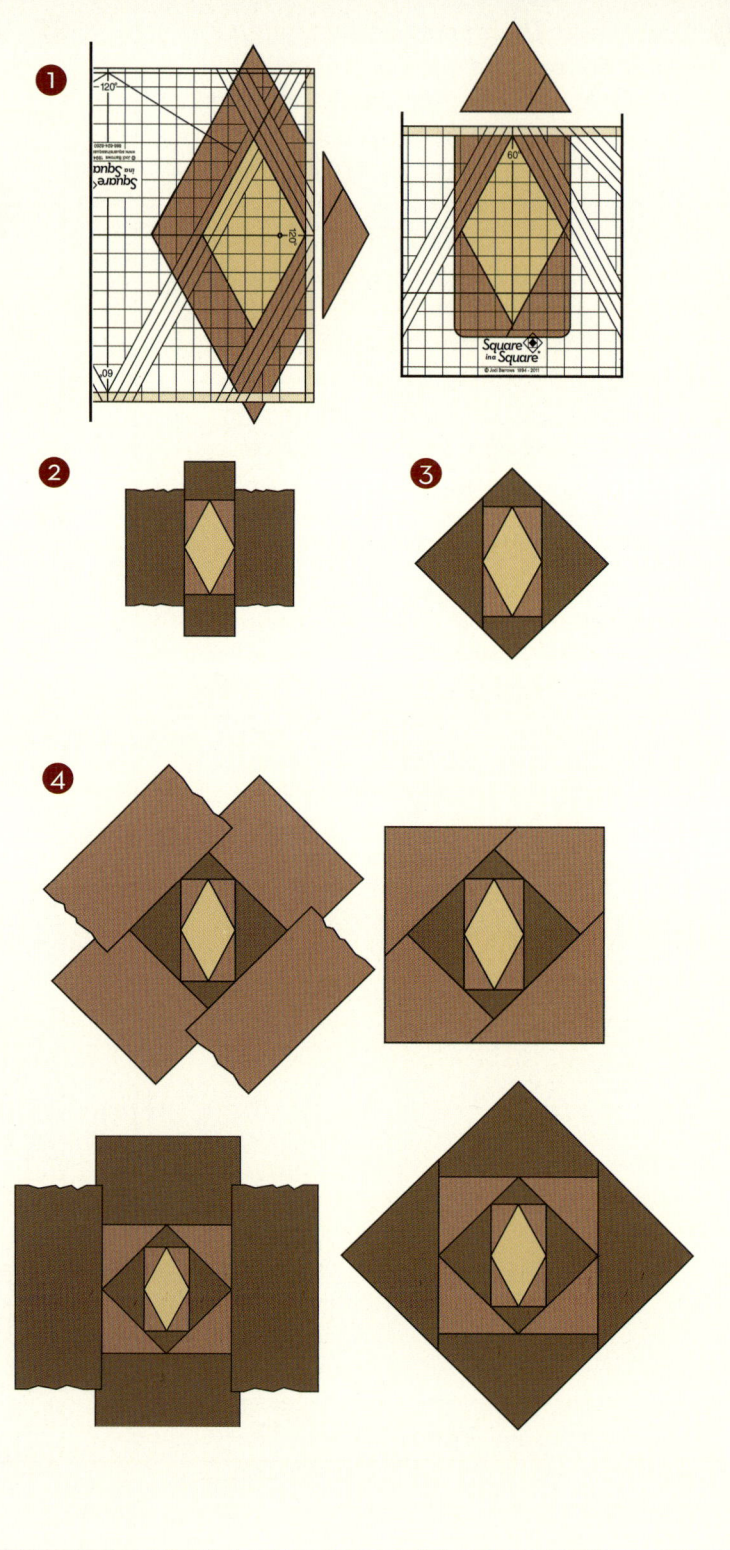

Option 22—The Diamond Twist

You can twist the center of the **Basic Diamond** by continuing to add strips in the same method and trimming each surround strip or round with the 60° angle on the ruler until you have the size that is required.

① Sew a **Basic Diamond** and trim as you would an Option 7, leaving ¼" seam allowance on all four sides.

② Sew a second round of surround strips to your center rectangle. Match any corner of the new rectangle with the 60° angle on the ruler. Trim all four corners as you would an Option 1 leaving a ¼" seam allowance.

Hint: when **trimming** this block **always use the same side of the 60° angle**. This will make the blocks all twist in the same direction.

③ Continue adding surround strips and trimming with one side of the 60° angle until your block is the desired size.

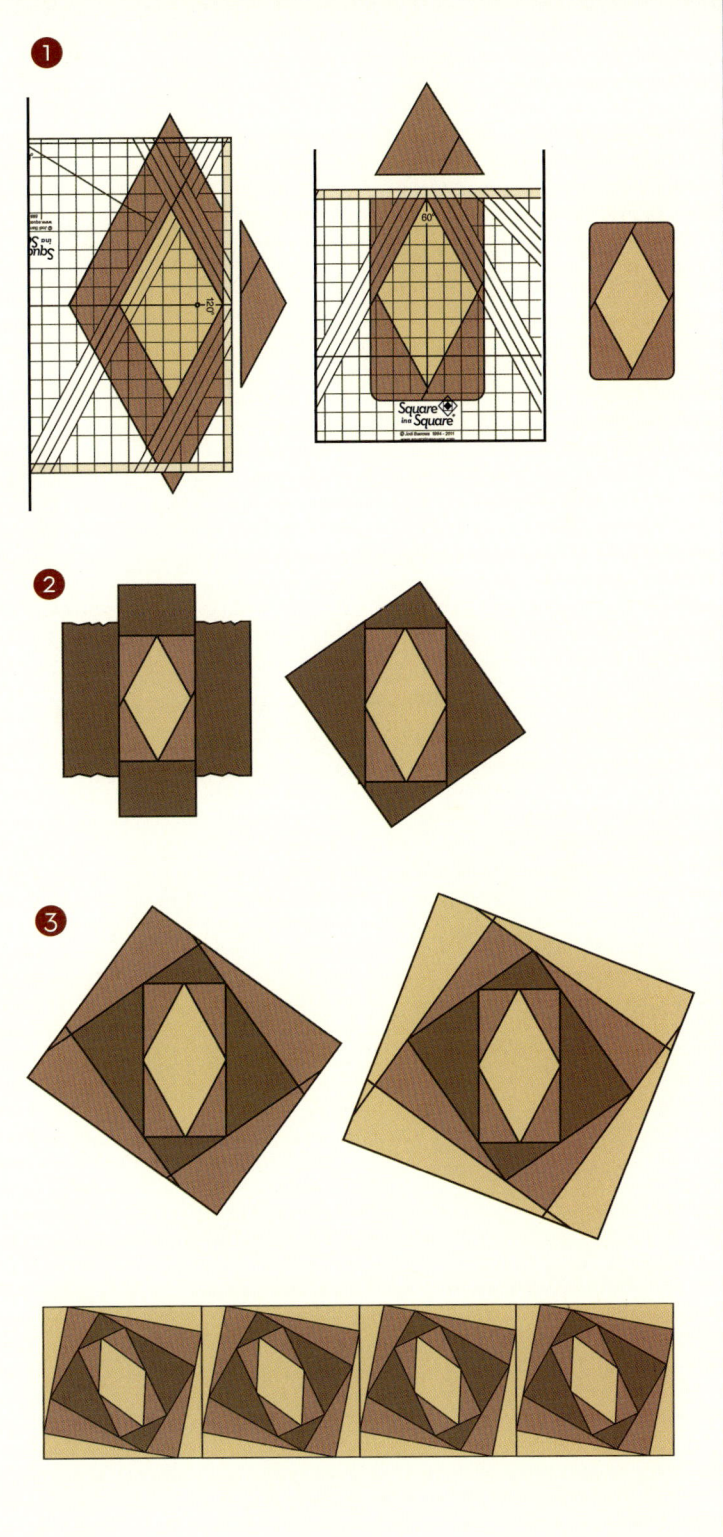

27

Option 23—The Diamond Pineapple

The pineapple block can be confusing because we don't really have any rules. You may use any size center diamond and any size of surround strips. For a traditional pineapple the strips will stay the same width as you sew around the center. The option is trimmed by using all three angles on the ruler. When you get the block size you need, just stop adding strips and finish out the four corners.

1. Sew a **Basic Diamond** and trim as you would an Option 7, leaving ¼" seam allowance on all four sides.
2. Sew a second round of surround strips to your new center rectangle. Match any corner of the new rectangle with the 90° angle on the ruler. Trim all four corners as you would an Option 7, leaving a ¼" seam allowance.
3. Continue adding surround strips and trimming with one side of the 90° angle until you start to have holes in the corner of your block. This happens about the third row of surround strips. You now will start creating eight sides of the block. When trimming the block at this point you will only use the edge of the ruler as a straight cut.
4. Continuing sewing the surround strips alternating between the two sets of four.

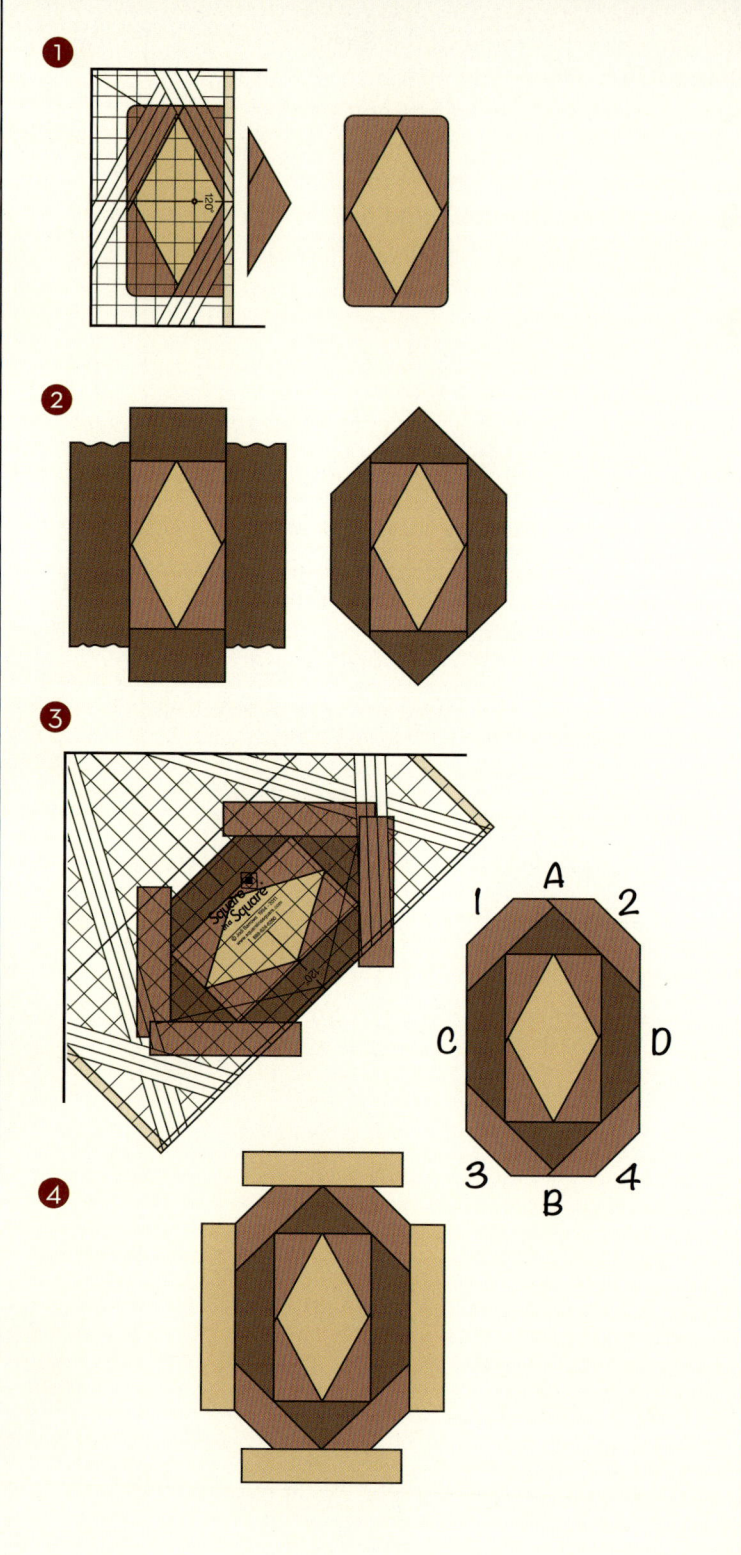

Option 24—Wagon Spokes

You can create multiple triangle units by cutting the diamond in half diagonally once.

① Sew a **Basic Diamond** and trim as you would an Option 7, leaving ¼" seam allowance on all four sides. Cut the diamond in half diagonally using the edge of the ruler, creating two triangle shapes.

② There are many ways to use this unit. Borders are great by using multiple colors. When using the charts; find the size you are looking for in the cut or sewn size from the first two columns. Then follow along horizontally for diamond strip size and additional strip sizes to complete the option. The block sewn size is an approximate size. This will help you get in the right ballpark to create the required size.

③ The circles that these create are quite easy and fun to make. You can sew them together with the north or short sides even. This creates an open circle in the center. The circle block can be appliqued to the desired size of square. You will need 13 units, which would be 7 diamond centers.

Extenders can also be sewn on the end of the Option to make the circle unit square. When sewing extenders to the ends, I like to use a rectangle or strip and sew two at a time. This will sew quickly and accurately and have the best fabric use. I start at the ends and work my way to the center of the strip.

These extenders (rectangle strips) can be made wider which would give you more area around the outside edge of the circle. This changes the block size without changing the option size. With right sides together, lay the unit on the rectangle strip. Sew the short side onto the long side of the rectangle strip.

④ Press open and cut at the angle.

⑤ Completed unit with extenders.

Option 25—Long Legged Ladies

You can create multiple triangle units by cutting the diamond in half diagonally both directions.

① Sew a **Basic Diamond** and trim as you would an Option 7, leaving ¼" seam allowance on all four sides. To trim this rectangle into the new option, cut diagonally corner to corner twice, creating four units. With this option you create two different units.

② There are many ways to use these units. Borders are great. When figuring the size for unit 1, use the long side of the rectangle on the chart. When figuring the size for unit 2, use the short side of the rectangle on the chart. Always work with the sewn size when figuring borders.

③ The circles that these units create are quite easy and fun to make. Twelve units are required which is six diamond centers. To complete the circle, appliqué it onto a square. A circle can be applied to the center or use the reverse appliqué method.

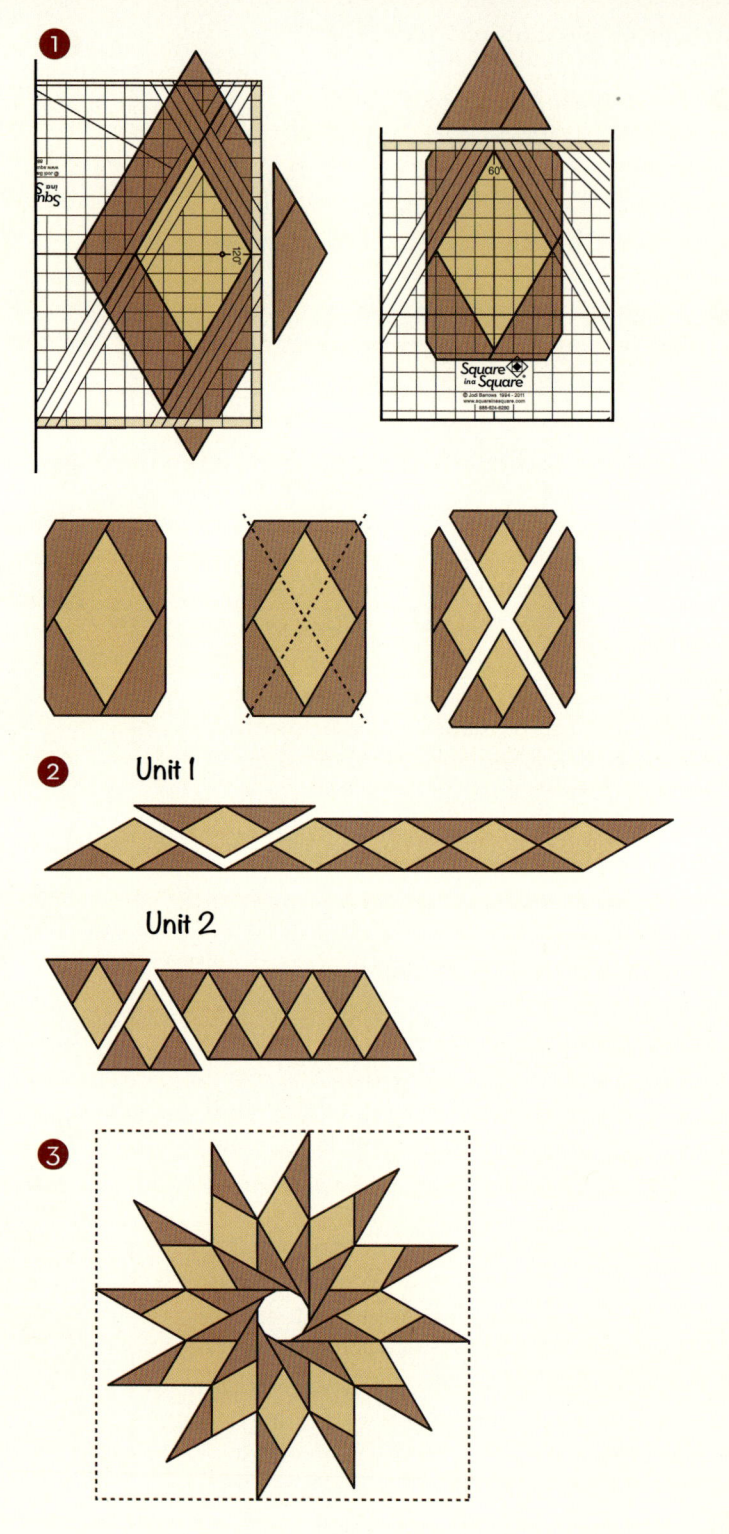

Option 25 (cont'd)

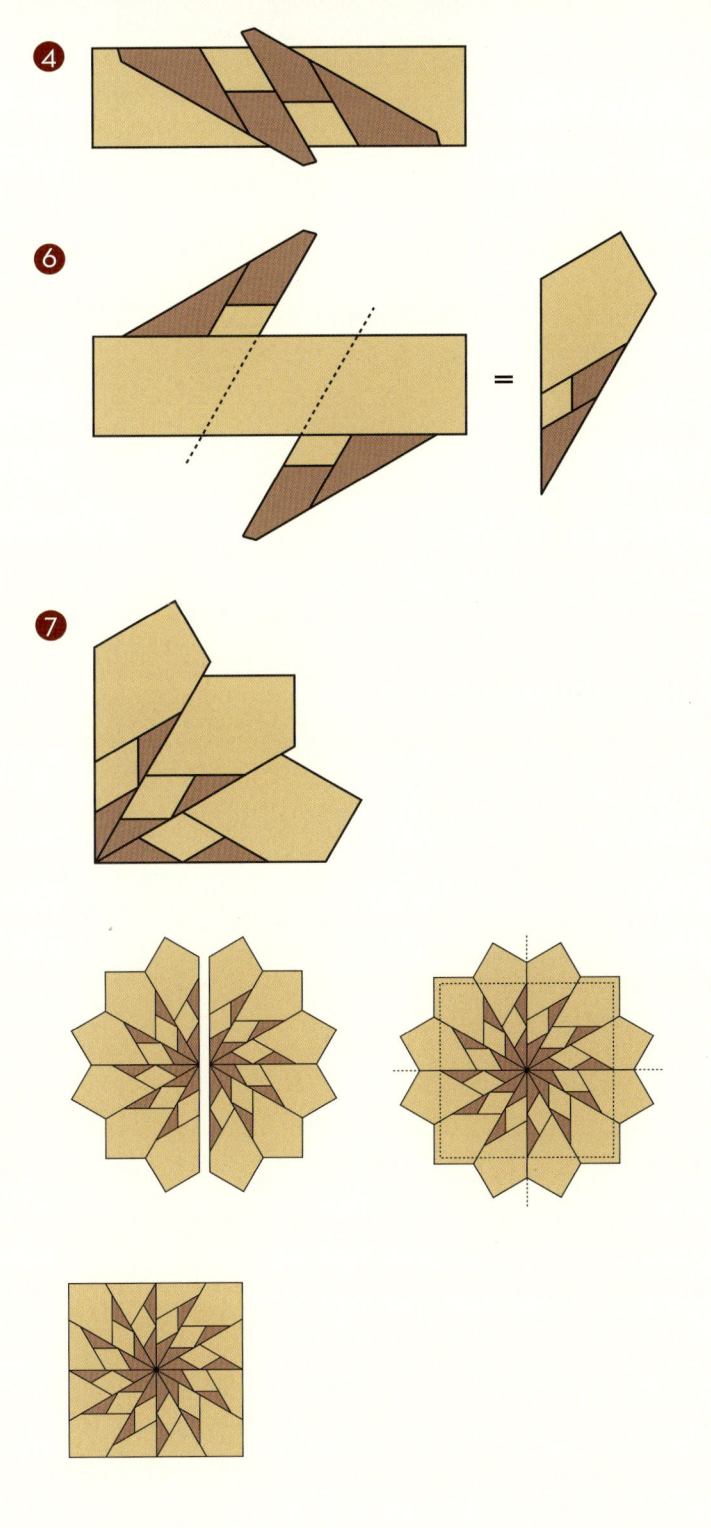

4. Extenders can also be sewn on the short side of each new unit. This makes the circle unit square for the final trim. When sewing extenders to the ends, I like to use a rectangle and sew two at a time. This sews quickly and accurately and has the best fabric use. Sew right sides together. *Hint*: you can make the block larger by making the extender rectangle wider.
5. The rectangle length needs to be the short side of the unit doubled and as wide as the long side of the unit divided in half.
6. Press open and cut.
7. You can sew the long units together with the center matching. This makes a starburst circle. Sew three units together four times. Sew the four sections to create the circle. Use a large square ruler and trim evenly into a square.

Option 25 (cont'd)

The other two units from this Option create a great tumbling star. Six units or three diamond centers are required for each star.

❽ Sew three units together for one half moon, repeat. To figure size of star refer to the chart.

❾ Sew the half moon shapes together flipping every other one to create a row. Then sew the rows together, matching the half moon shapes to the units above and below.

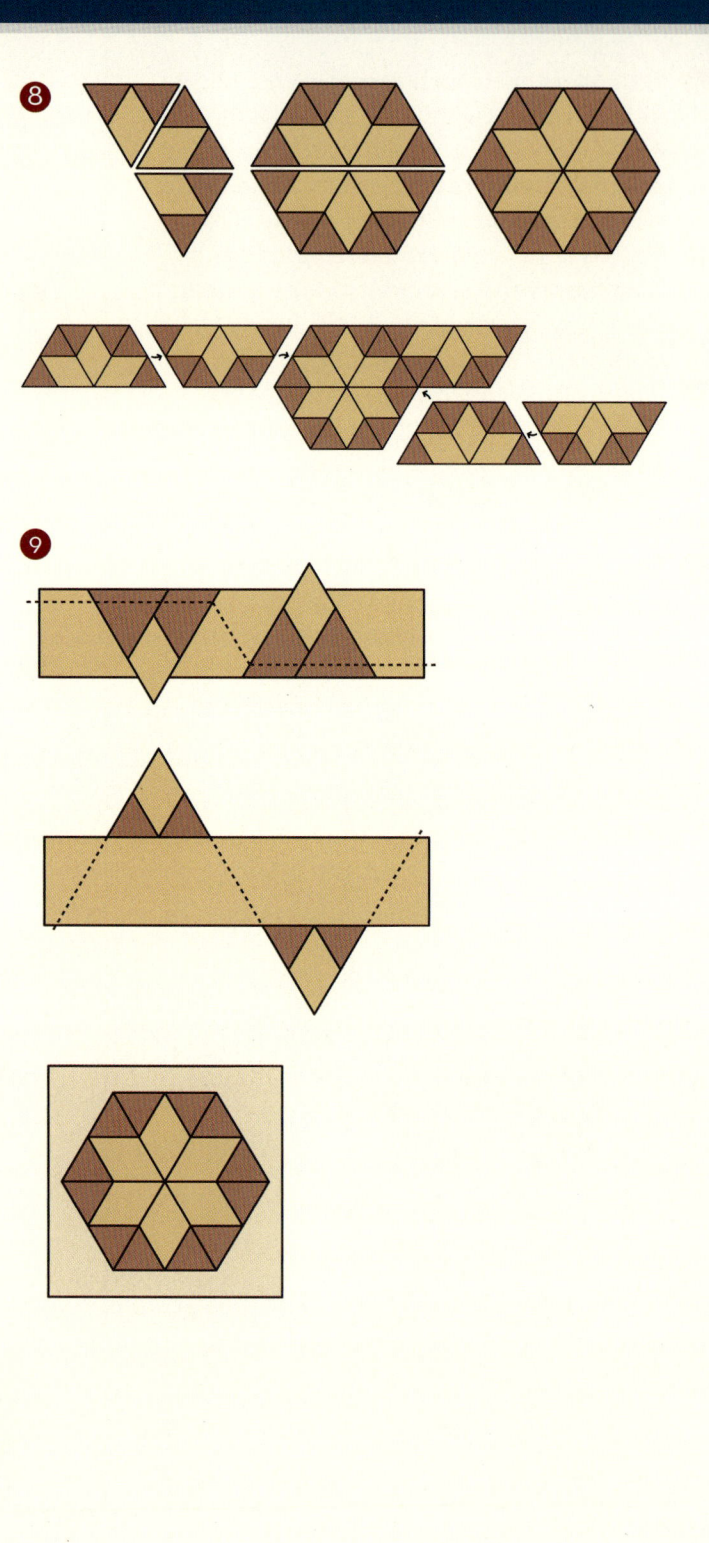

Option 26

1. Sew a **Basic Diamond** and trim as you would an Option 7, leaving ¼" seam allowance on all four sides.
2. Add a second row of surround strips to your new center rectangle.
3. Trim all four corners up to the point of the center rectangle. Trim is like an Option 4.
4. Trim into four units by cutting in half twice diagonally through the corners of the center rectangle.
5. Cutting sequences are Option #7 and #4. There are many ways to use the options. Borders are great from these two units. Refer to Options 24, 25 and 27 for more ideas and information.

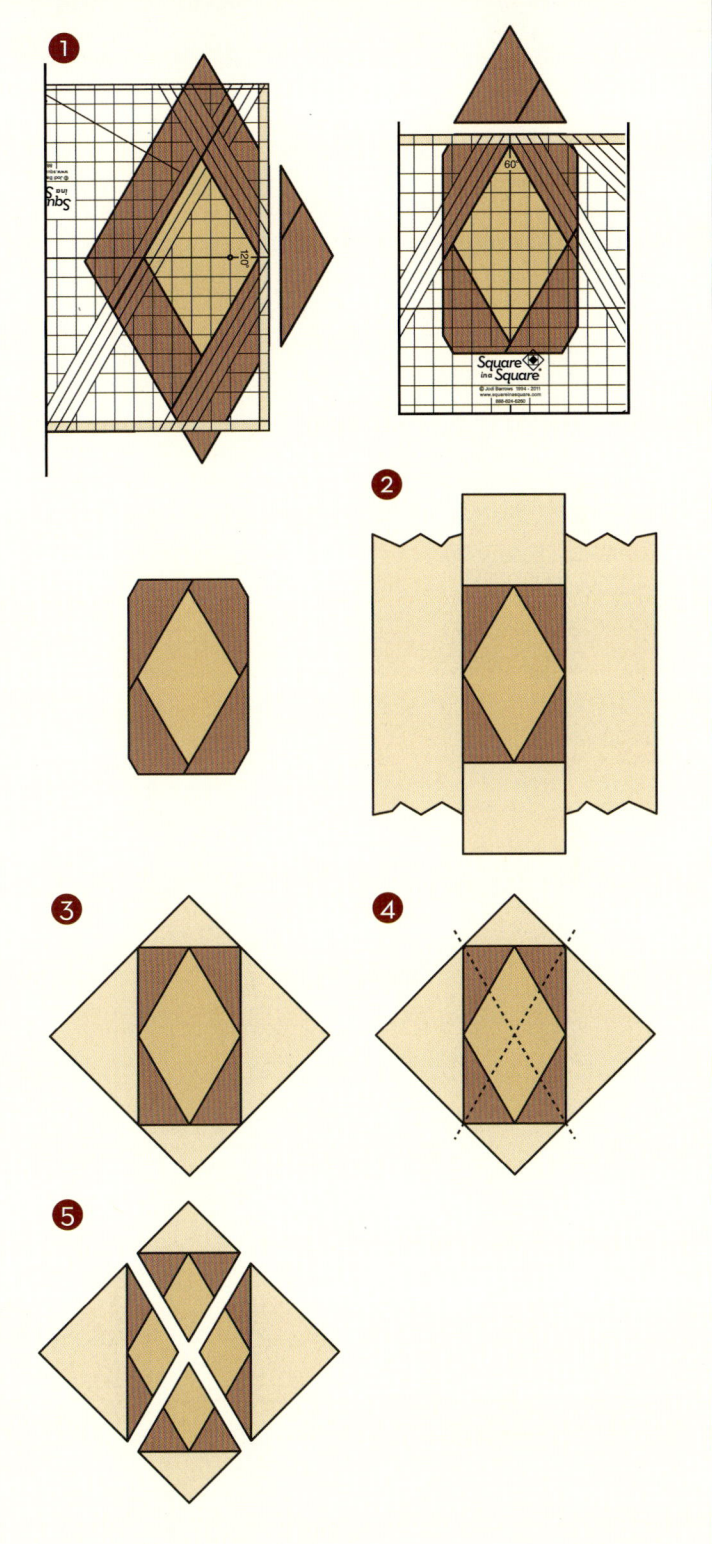

Option 27—Seven Sisters

1. Sew a **Basic Diamond** and trim as you would an Option 7.
2. Add a second row of surround strips to your new center rectangle. Trim all four corners up to the point of the center rectangle as you would an Option 4.
3. Add a third row of surround strips to your center square and trim, leaving a ¼" seam allowance as you would an Option 1. *Hint*: the blunt corners of the center rectangle should be a perfect ¼" opening.
4. Trim into four units by cutting in half twice diagonally through the ¼" seam allowance of the center rectangle, as shown.

There are many ways to use these options. Borders are great from both of the units.

QUICK TIP
cutting sequences are Options #7, #4, and #1

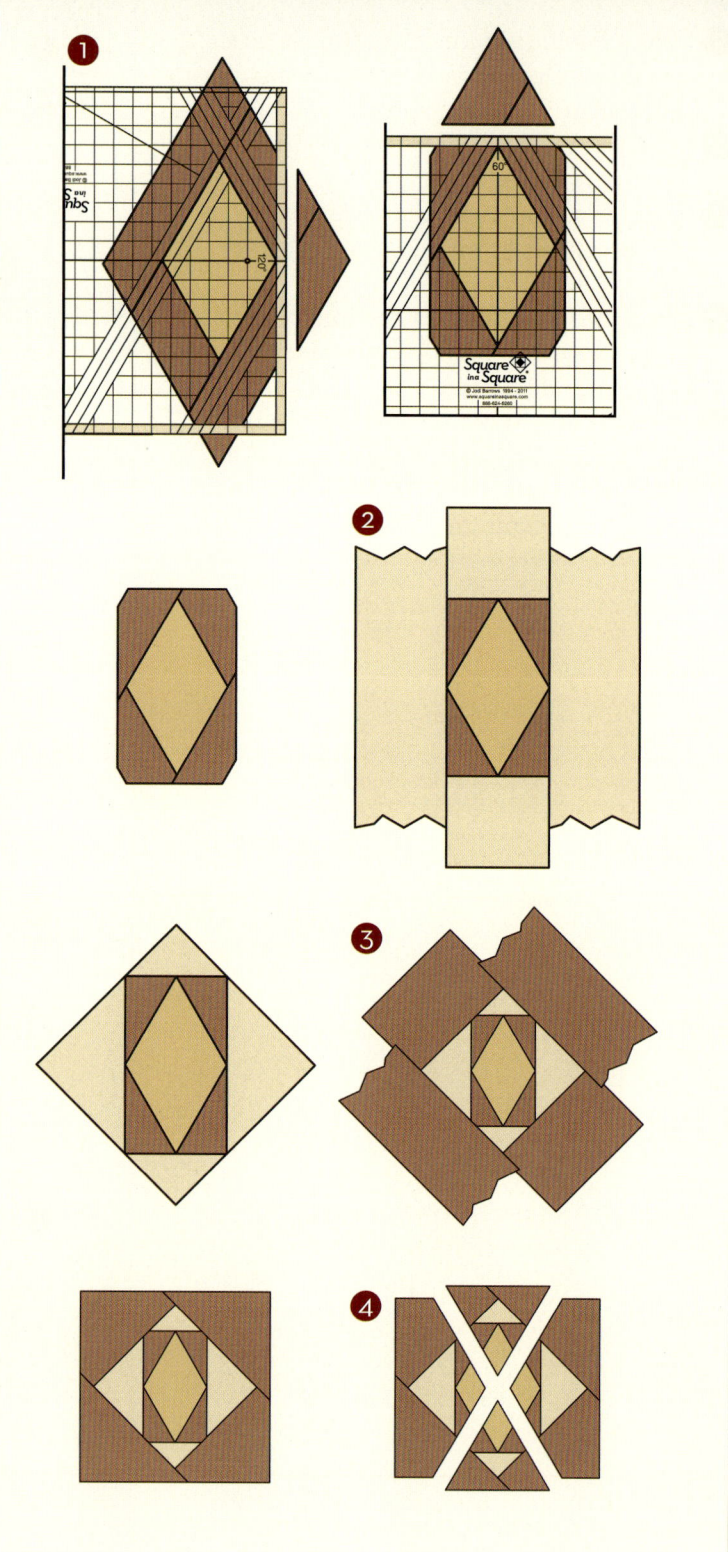

Option 27 (cont'd)

5. Larger side units may be squared up for easier application for a border.
6. These Option 27 units create beautiful borders when sewn side to side.
7. Sew the half moon shapes together, flipping every other one to create a row. Then, sew the rows together matching the half moon shapes to the units above and below.

Option 28—Looking Glass

1. Sew a **Basic Diamond** and trim as you would an Option 7, leaving ¼" seam allowance on all four sides.
2. Add a second row of surround strips to your new center rectangle. Trim all four corners as you would an Option 1, leaving a ¼" seam allowance on all four sides.
3. Add a third row of surround strips to your new center square. Trim all four corners as you would an Option 1, leaving a ¼" seam allowance.
4. Cutting sequences are Options 7, 1, and 1. Trim into four units by cutting in half twice diagonally from corner to corner, as shown.
5. There are many ways to use these options. Borders are great from both of the units or create unique blocks by sewing opposite triangle units together.

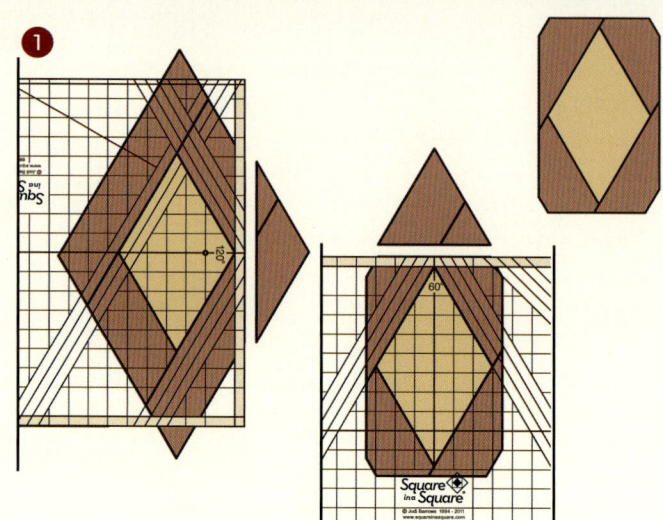

Option 29—The Instant Star

1. Sew a **Basic Diamond** and trim as an Option 18, leaving a ¼" seam allowance on the 60° angles and a ⅛" seam allowance on the 120° angles.
2. Add a second row of surround strips to your new center rectangle. Trim all four corners as you would an Option 1, leaving a ¼" seam allowance.
3. Cut in half, corner to corner laying the edge of the ruler across the unit.
4. This option is great for borders as well as blocks.
5. Any triangle option works well on the outside edge of any block.

Hint: Make sure that when you cut in half, that you cut through the blunt corners of the inside diamond.

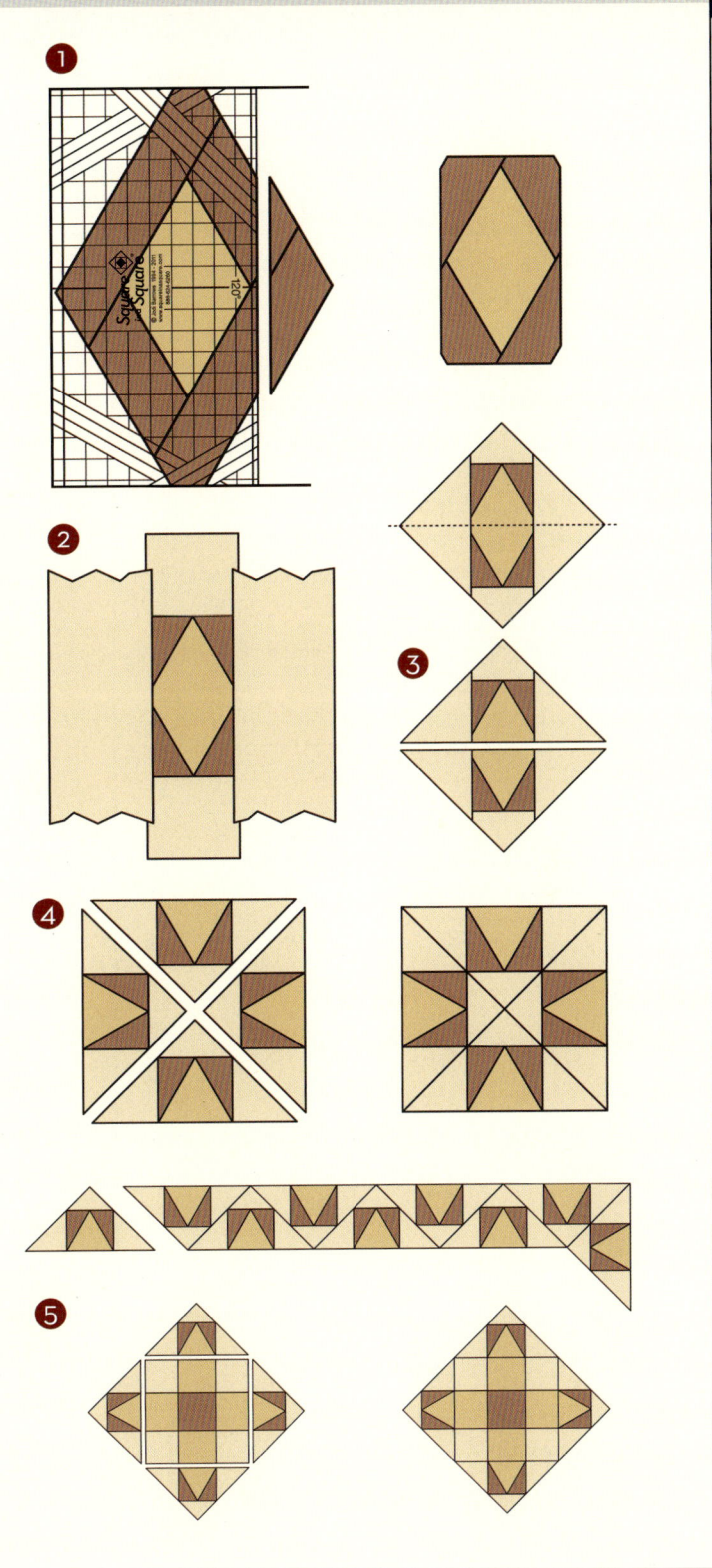

QUICK TIP
cutting sequences are Options #18 and #1

Option 30—Father Goose

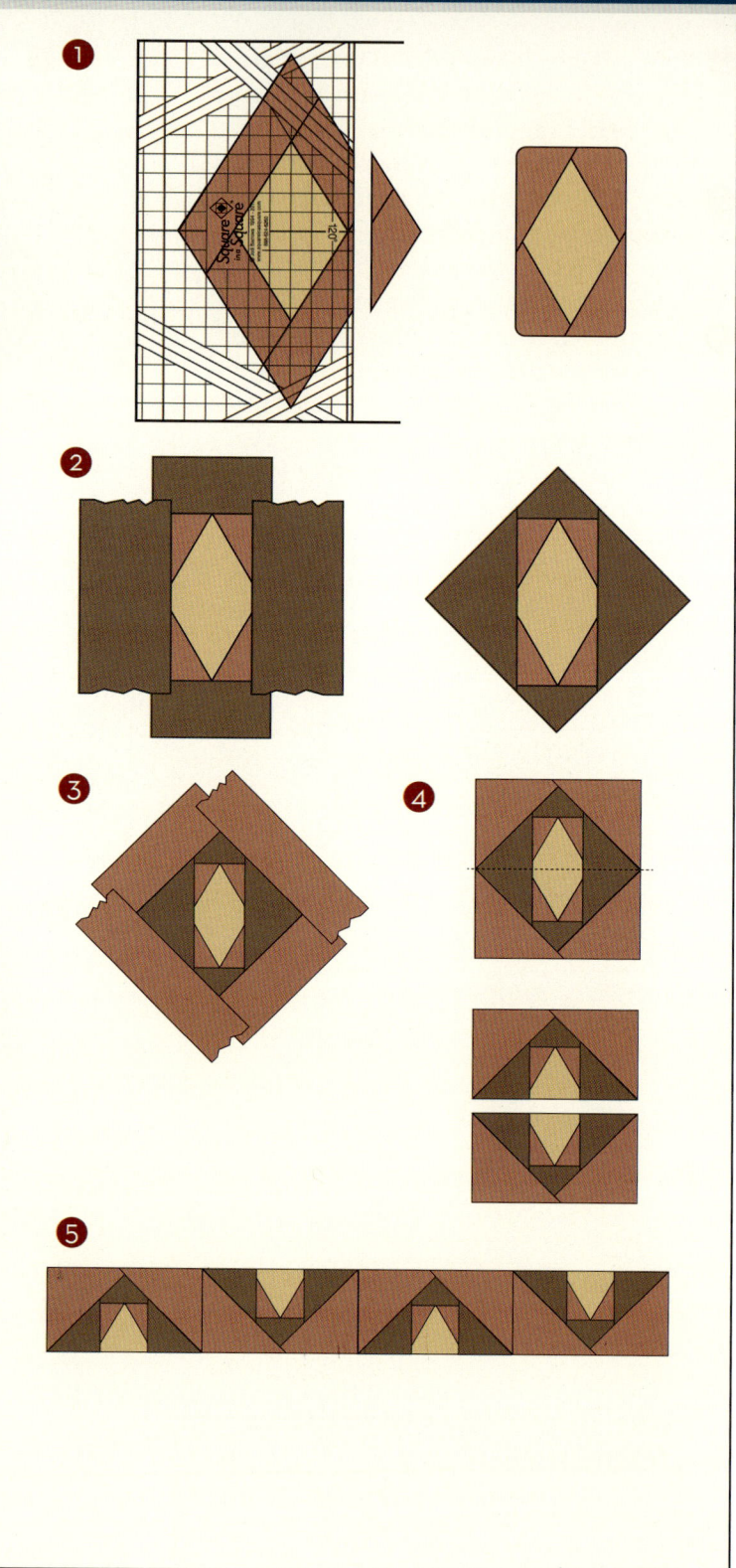

1. Sew a **Basic Diamond** and trim as you would an Option 18, leaving a ¼" seam allowance on the 60° angles and a ⅛" seam allowance on the 120° angles.
2. Add a second row of surround strips to your new center rectangle. Trim all four corners as you would an Option 1, leaving a ¼" seam allowance.
3. Add a third row of surround strips to your new center square. Trim all four corners as you would an Option 3.
   Hint: When trimming in Step 3, watch carefully for the Option 3, Texas 2-Step trim. It should be horizontal to the ⅛" trim from Step 1.
4. Cut in half horizontally through the side of the diamond, as shown.
5. This option is great for borders as well as blocks.

> **QUICK TIP**
> *cutting sequences are Options #18, #1, and #3*

Option 31

1. Sew a **Basic Diamond** and trim as you would an Option 18, leaving a ¼" seam allowance on the 60° angles and a ⅛" seam allowance on the 120° angles.
2. Add a second row of surround strips to your new center rectangle. Trim all four corners up to the point of the center rectangle as you would an Option 4.
3. Add a third row of surround strips to your center square. Trim all four corners as you would an Option 1, leaving a ¼" seam allowance.
4. This option is great as a setting block, borders, corner squares and all by itself. Manipulate the colors for extravagant quilts.

Hint: This Option creates a blunted look on the center rectangle unit.

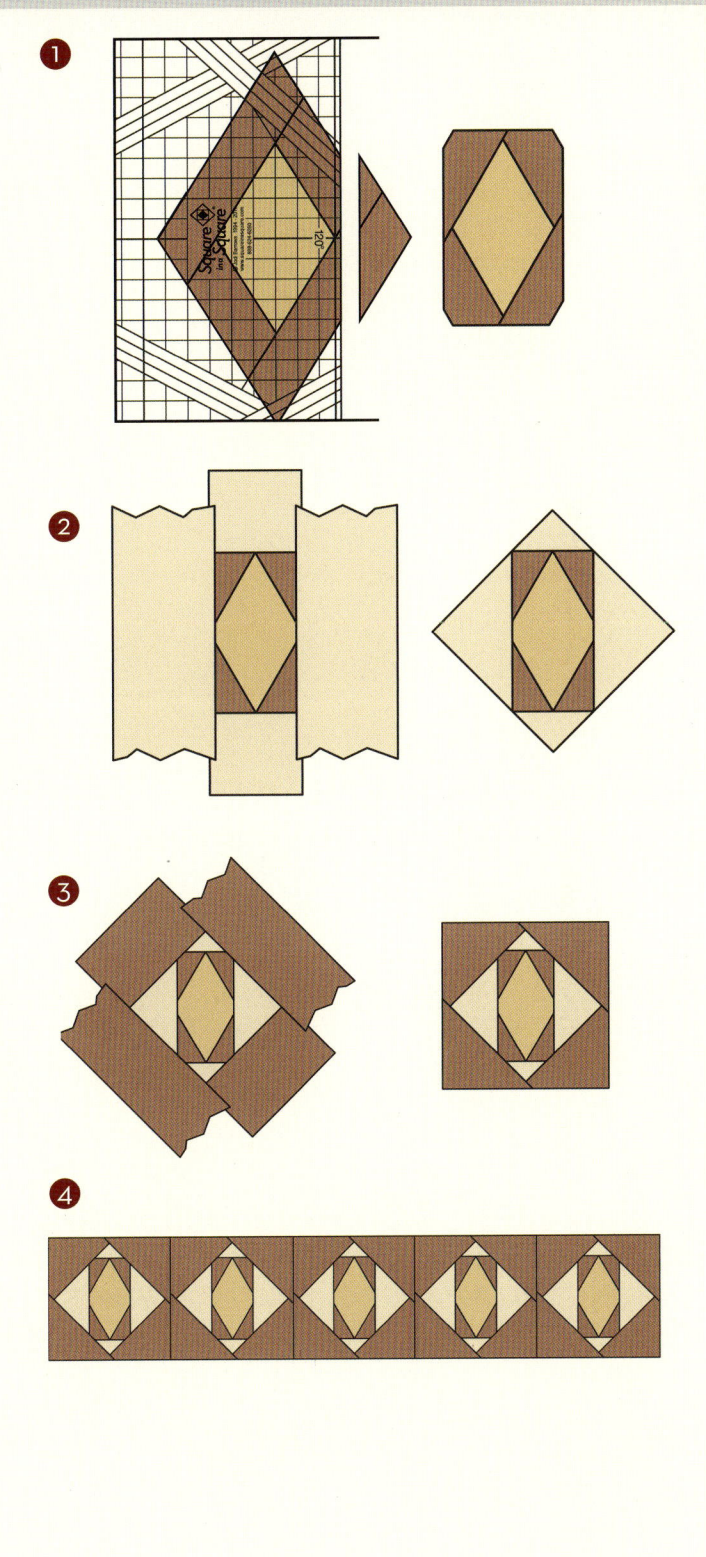

QUICK TIP
cutting sequences are Options #18, #4 and #1

Option 32—Slim Jim

1. Sew a **Basic Diamond** and trim as you would an Option 18, leaving a ¼" seam allowance on the 60° angles and a ⅛" seam allowance on the 120° angles.
2. Add a second row of surround strips to your new center rectangle. Trim all four corners up to the point of the center rectangle as you would an Option 4.
3. Add a third row of surround strips to your center square. Trim all four corners as you would an Option 3.
4. Cut in half corner to corner through the side of the diamond as shown.
5. This unit works well as building blocks and for border units. Try using horizontally and vertically.

QUICK TIP
cutting sequences are Options #18, #4, and #3

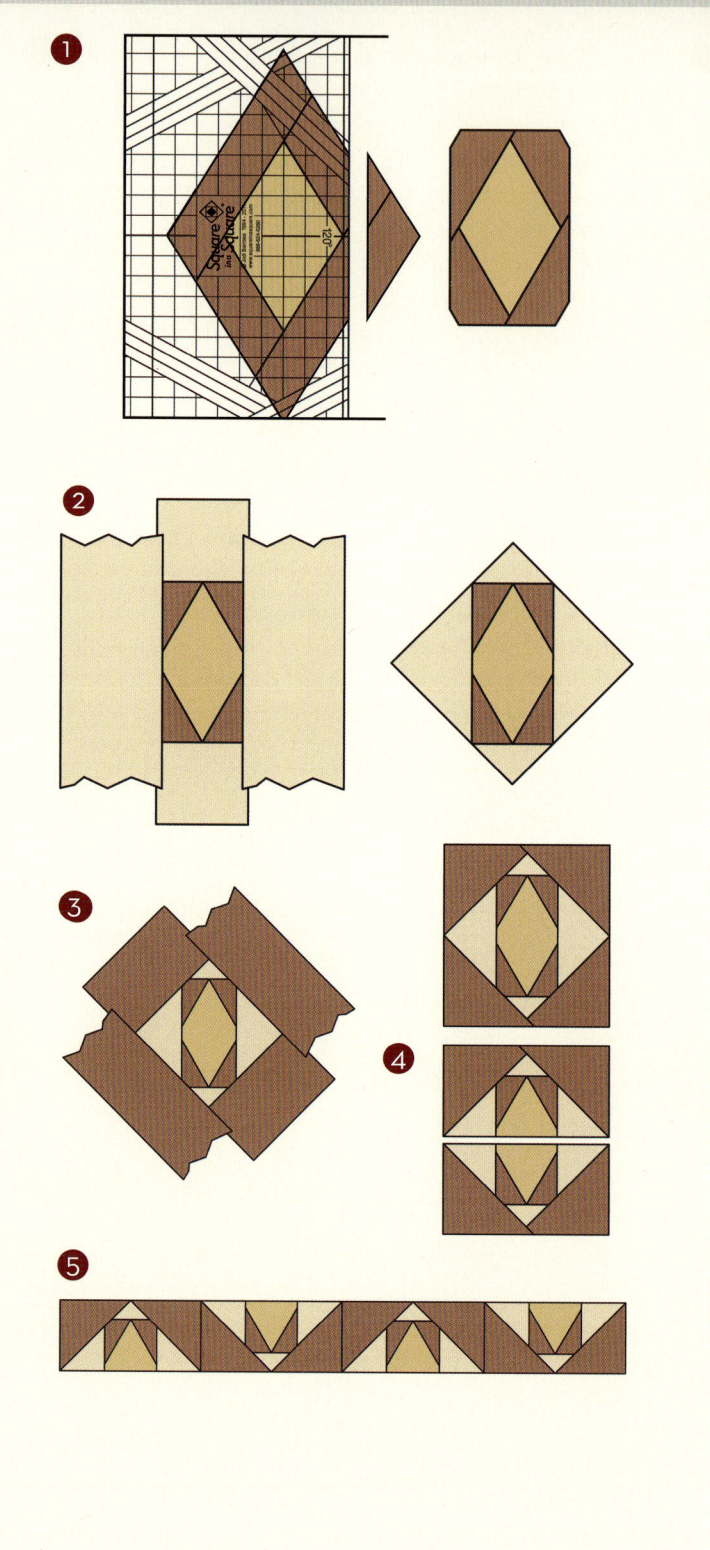

Option 33—The Snowball Block

1. Sew a **Basic Diamond** and trim as you would an Option 19.
   To trim Option 19 place the diamond vertically. Trim both 60° angles, by dragging the 60° angle on the ruler down across the set of seams, one set of lines. After trimming this will leave a blunted edge across the top and bottom points. *Hint*: the blunt 60° area should be a perfect ¼" opening.
2. Trim both 120° angles of the diamond by placing the 120° angle on the ruler with the ⅛" seam allowance at the point of the center diamond. This will leave ⅛" of fabric on the outside point of the diamond. This is necessary for acquiring the perfect point after the unit is cut and resewn.
3. When this option is sewn into the block or used as a block, it creates a snowball look, with thin triangles. It is great as a confetti look or as a border. When rows are sewn together, it creates a floating diamond.

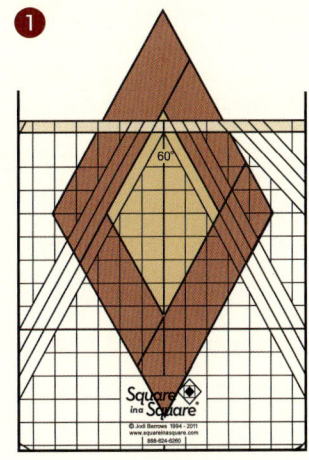

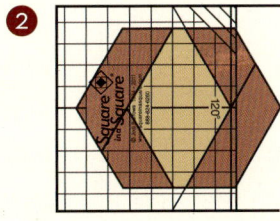
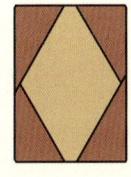

Option 34—Halloween Eyes

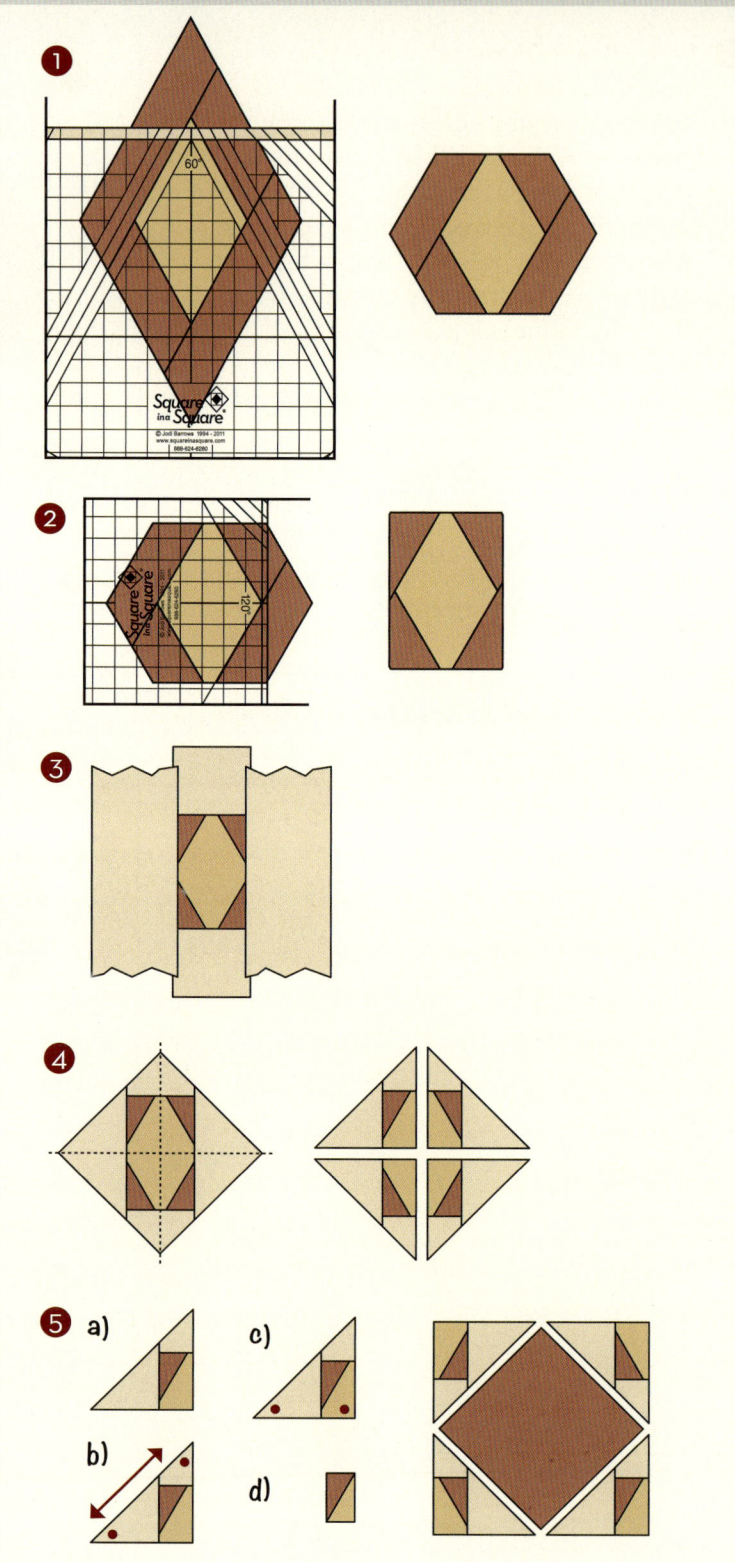

1. Sew a **Basic Diamond** and trim as you would an Option 19. To trim Option 19 place the diamond vertically. Trim both 60° angles, by dragging the 60° angle on the ruler down across the set of seams, one set of lines. After trimming this will leave a blunted edge across the top and bottom points.
Hint: the blunt 60° should be a perfect ¼" opening.
2. Trim both 120° angles of the diamond by placing the 120° angle on the ruler with the ⅛" seam allowance at the point of the center diamond. This will leave ⅛" of fabric on the outside point of the diamond. This is necessary for acquiring the perfect point after the unit is cut and resewn.
3. Add a second row of surround strips to your new center rectangle. Trim all four corners as you would an Option 1, leaving a ¼" seam allowance.
4. Cut in half horizontally and vertically through the diamond, as shown.
5. These tips will help you use the charts. Remember you have 2 mirror units.
   a) Cut unit — arrows show outside angle.
   b) If you want the outside angle of the option to fit the edge of a new square block, use this measurement. Add ⅞" to this sewn measurement.
   c) If you want the inside angle of the option to fit the edge of a new square or block, use this measurement.
   d) If you have drawn your pattern on graph paper, this is the sewn size of the rectangle eye. This may be where you need to start to figure the size.

> **QUICK TIP**
> *cutting sequences are Options #19 and #1*

Option 35—Jodi's Favorite Corner Unit

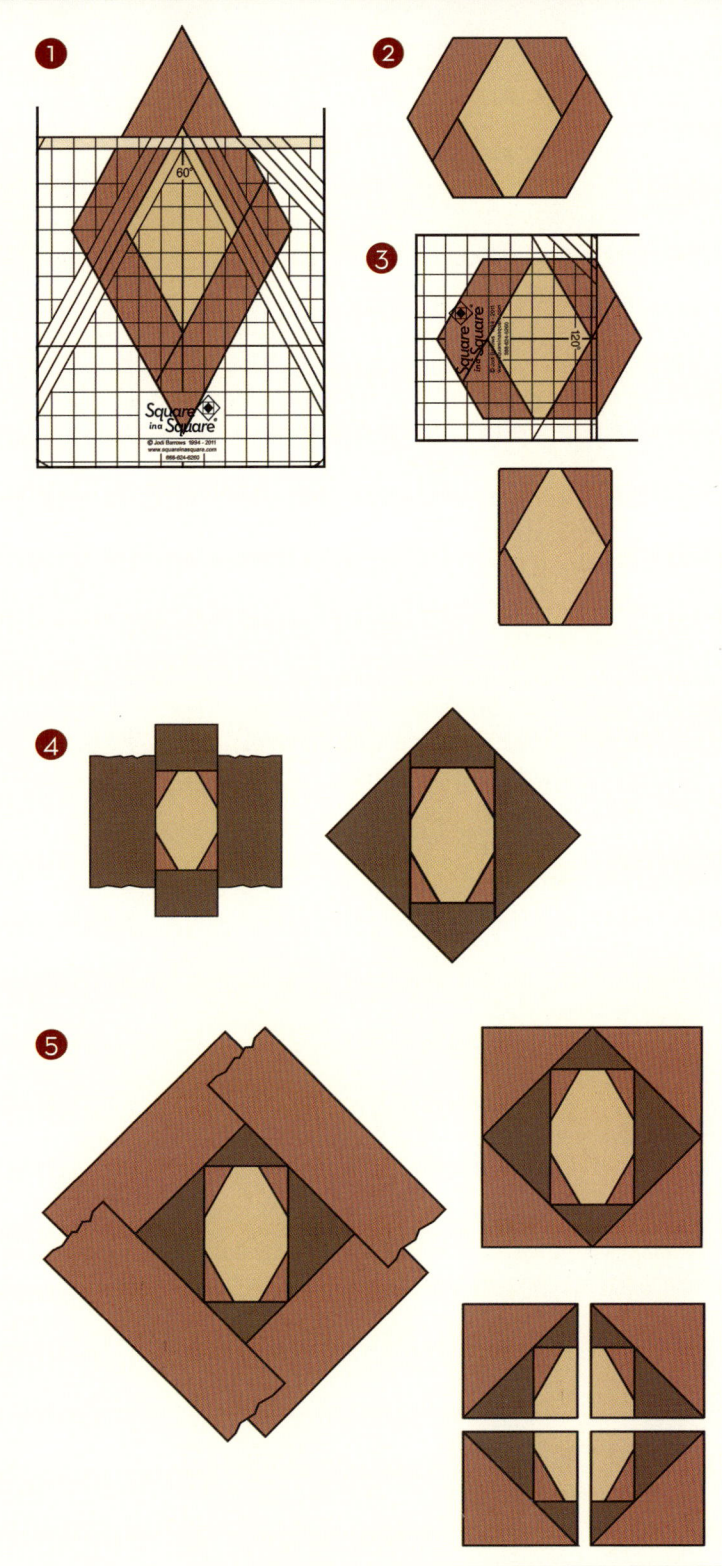

1. Sew a **Basic Diamond** and trim as you would an Option 19.
2. To trim Option 19 place the diamond vertically. Trim both 60° angles, by dragging the 60° angle on the ruler down across the set of seams, one set of lines. After trimming this will leave a blunted edge across the top and bottom points. *Hint:* the blunt 60° should be a perfect ¼" opening.
3. Trim both 120° angles of the diamond by placing the 120° angle on the ruler with the ⅛" seam allowance at the point of the center diamond. This will leave ⅛" of fabric on the outside point of the diamond. This is necessary for acquiring the perfect point after the unit is cut and resewn.
4. Add a second row of surround strips to your new center rectangle. Trim all four corners, leaving a ¼" seam allowance as you would an Option 1.
5. Add a third row of surround strips to your center square. Trim all four corners as you would an Option 4. Cut in half horizontally and vertically through the diamond, as shown.

QUICK TIP
cutting sequences are Options #19, #1 and #4

Option 36—Rooftop Triangle

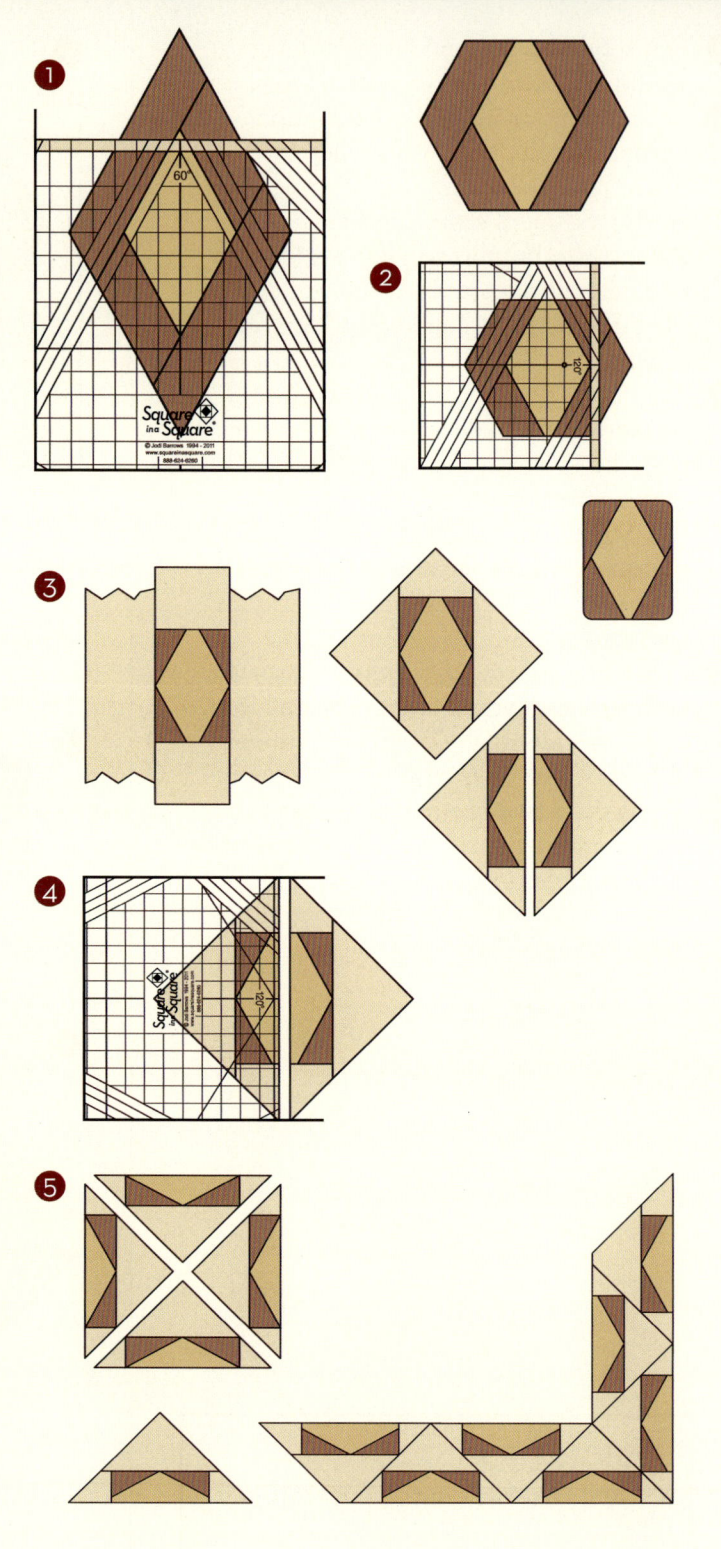

1. Sew a **Basic Diamond** and trim as you would an Option 20. To trim Option 20 place the diamond vertically. Trim both 60 angles, by dragging the 60° angle on the ruler down across the set of seams, one set of lines. After trimming this will leave a blunted edge across the top and bottom.
   Hint: the blunt 60° should be a perfect ¼" opening.
2. Trim both 120° angles of the diamond by placing the 120° angle on the ruler with the ¼" seam allowance at the point of the center diamond. This will leave ¼" of fabric on the outside point of the diamond, similar to the Option 7 diamond. This is necessary for acquiring the perfect point after the unit is cut and resewn.
3. Add a second row of surround strips to your new center rectangle. Trim all four corners as you would an Option 1, leaving a ¼" seam allowance.
4. Cut in half vertically through the tip of the diamond, as shown.
5. Borders and stars are my favorite for this option.

QUICK TIP
cutting sequences are Options #20 and #1

Option 37—Granny Goose

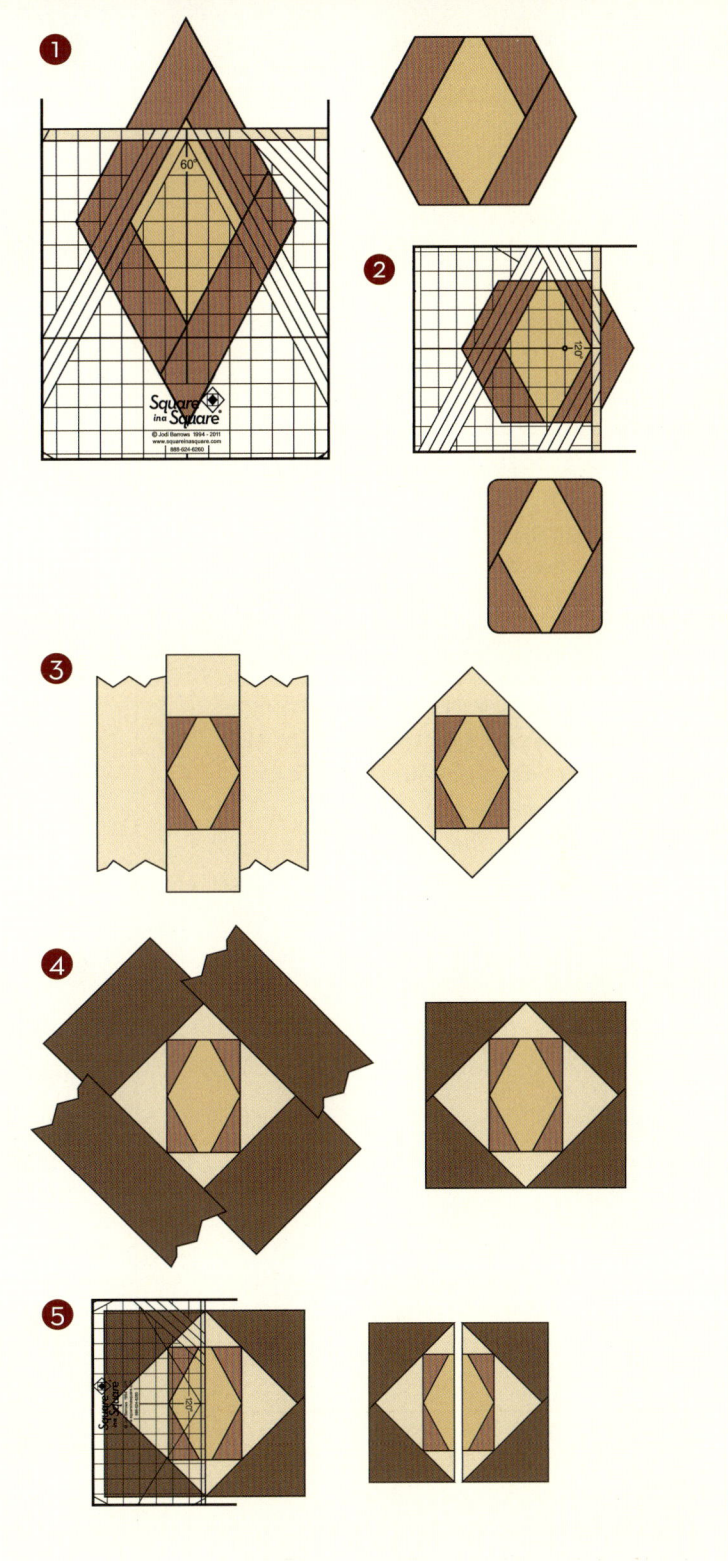

1. Sew a **Basic Diamond** and trim as you would an Option 20. To trim Option 20 place the diamond vertically. Trim both 60 angles, by dragging the 60° angle on the ruler down across the set of seams, one set of lines. After trimming this will leave a blunted edge across the top and bottom.
   Hint: the blunt 60° should be a perfect ¼" opening.
2. Trim both 120° angles of the diamond by placing the 120° angle on the ruler with the ¼" seam allowance at the point of the center diamond. This will leave ¼" of fabric on the outside point of the diamond, similar to the Option 7 diamond. This is necessary for acquiring the perfect point after the unit is cut and resewn.
3. Add a second row of surround strips to your new center rectangle. Trim all four corners as you would an Option 1, leaving a ¼" seam allowance.
4. Add a third row of surround strips to your center square. Trim as you would an Option 3.
5. Watch carefully when trimming on the third row as the blunt diamond area needs to match with the Texas 2-Step trim of Option 3.

QUICK TIP
cutting sequences are Options #20, #1 and #3

Option 38

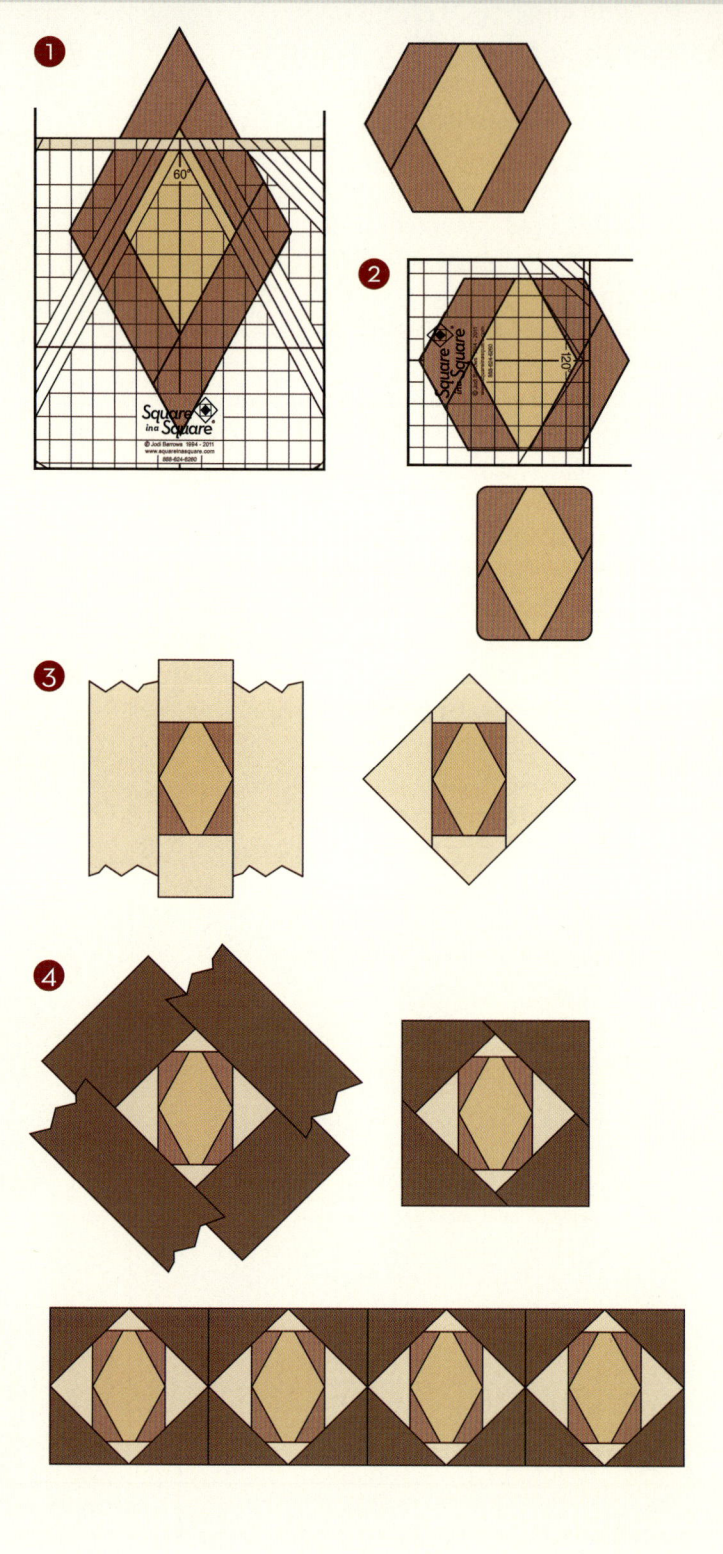

① Sew a **Basic Diamond** and trim as you would an Option 20. To trim Option 20 place the diamond vertically. Trim both 60° angles, by dragging the 60° angle on the ruler down across the set of seams, one set of lines. After trimming this will leave a blunted edge across the top and bottom of the diamond.
Hint: the blunt 60° should be a perfect ¼" opening.

② Trim both 120° angles of the diamond by placing the 120° angle on the ruler with the ¼" seam allowance at the point of the center diamond. This will leave ¼" of fabric on the outside point of the diamond, similar to the Option 7 diamond. This is necessary for acquiring the perfect point after the unit is cut and resewn.

③ Add a second row of surround strips to your new center rectangle. Trim all four corners as you would an Option 1, leaving a ¼" seam allowance.

④ Add a third row of surround strips to your center square. Trim all four corners as you would an Option 1, leaving a ¼" seam allowance.

QUICK TIP
cutting sequences are Options #20, #1 and #3

Option 39—Trumpet Square

1. Determine what size you would like your finished trumpet square to be and multiply by 2. This will give you the size of diamond you need. Sew a **Basic Diamond**.
   Place the Square in a Square® ruler on your **Basic Diamond** aligning the 120° grid line with the edge of your diamond at either 60° point. Trim up to the point of the diamond.
2. Rotate or "swing" the ruler clockwise to align the 120° line with the other edge of the same 60° point. Trim up to the point. Repeat for the other 60° point of the diamond.
3. Cut the unit in half horizontally from tip to tip as shown.
4. Cut several strips the same width as the surround strips used for the **Basic Diamond**. Sew the diamond halves, right sides together, along this strip or "leg", leaving a thumb space between each unit. Cut apart and press open with seams out towards the leg.

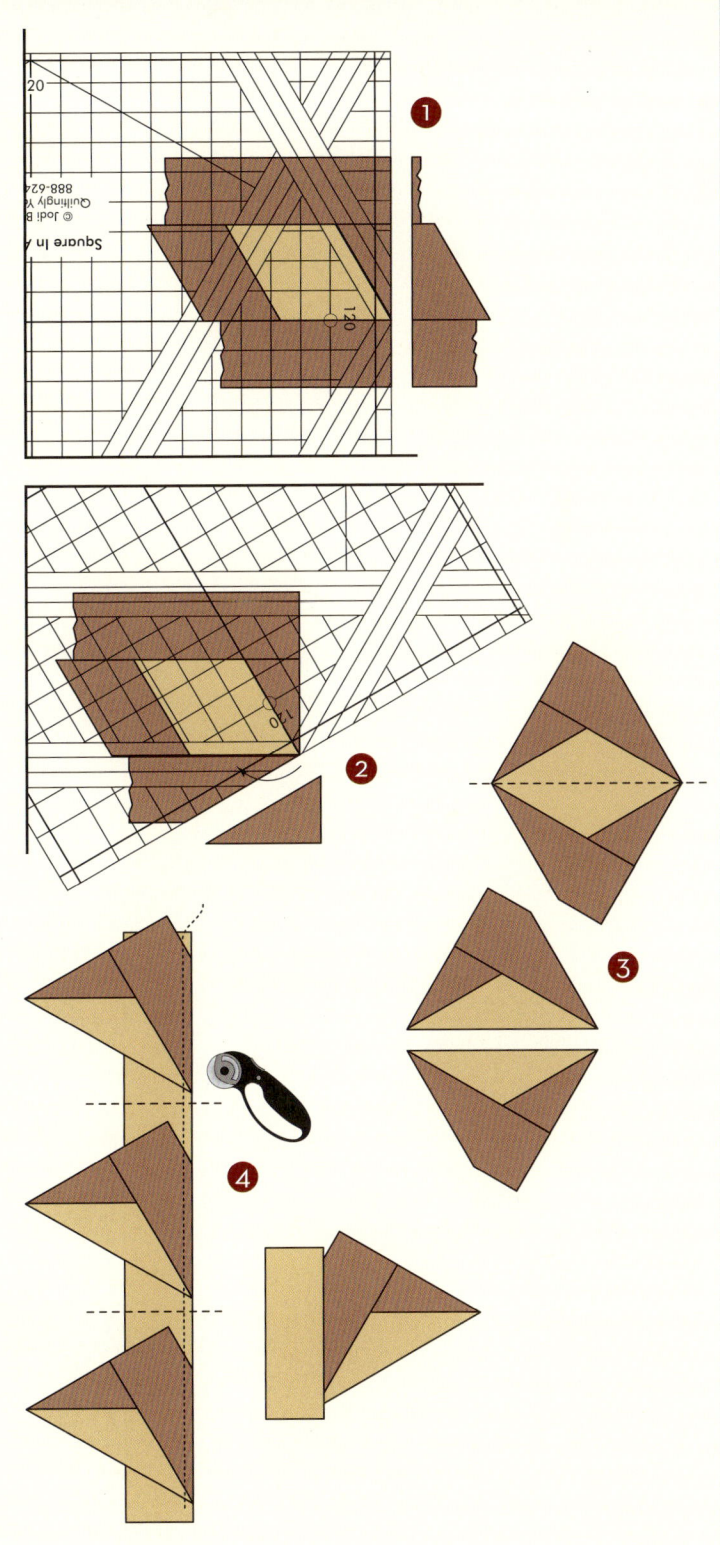

Option 39 (cont'd)

5. Repeat Step 4 with the opposite side of the unit.
6. Trim the edges of the unit, leaving a ¼" seam allowance at each point.
7. Align the 120° point of the ruler with the center of the diamond and trim, leaving a ¼" seam allowance.

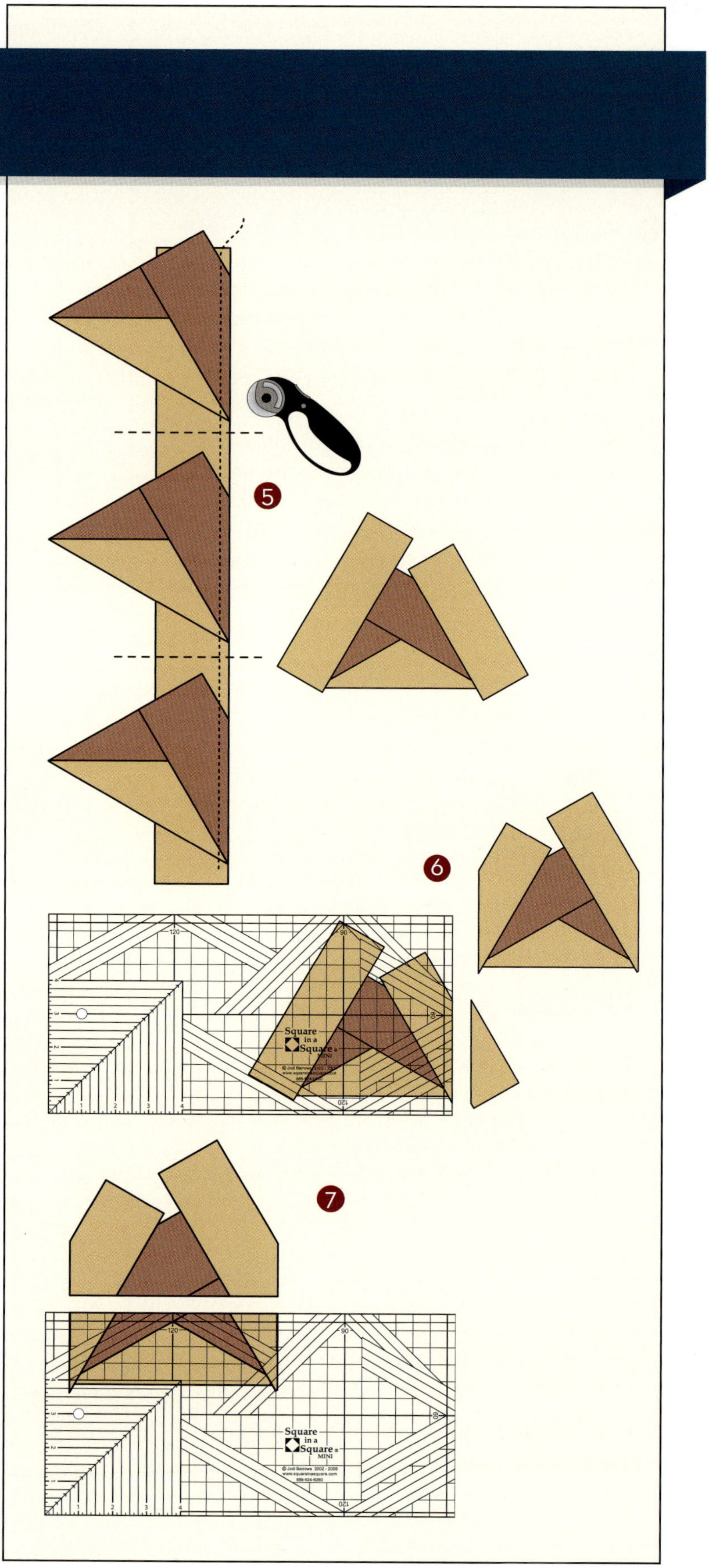

Option 39 (cont'd)

8. Place the Square in Square in a Square® Mini R5 ruler over the unit and align the left and bottom edge with the desired cut size of your trumpet square. The 45° line of the ruler should run through the narrow point of your trumpet. The open end, or top side and right side, should be the exact same width. Repeat on the opposite side for the second trumpet square. One diamond will yield enough trumpet squares to make a four-pointed star.

9. To get a bonus piece from your unit, measure the width and divide by three. Place ruler over the unit and align the left and bottom edge using this measurement. The 45° line of the ruler should run through the narrow point of your trumpet. The open end, or top side and right side, should be the exact same width.

10. Repeat on the opposite side for the second trumpet square. You now also have the center piece that can be used for designing blocks or borders.

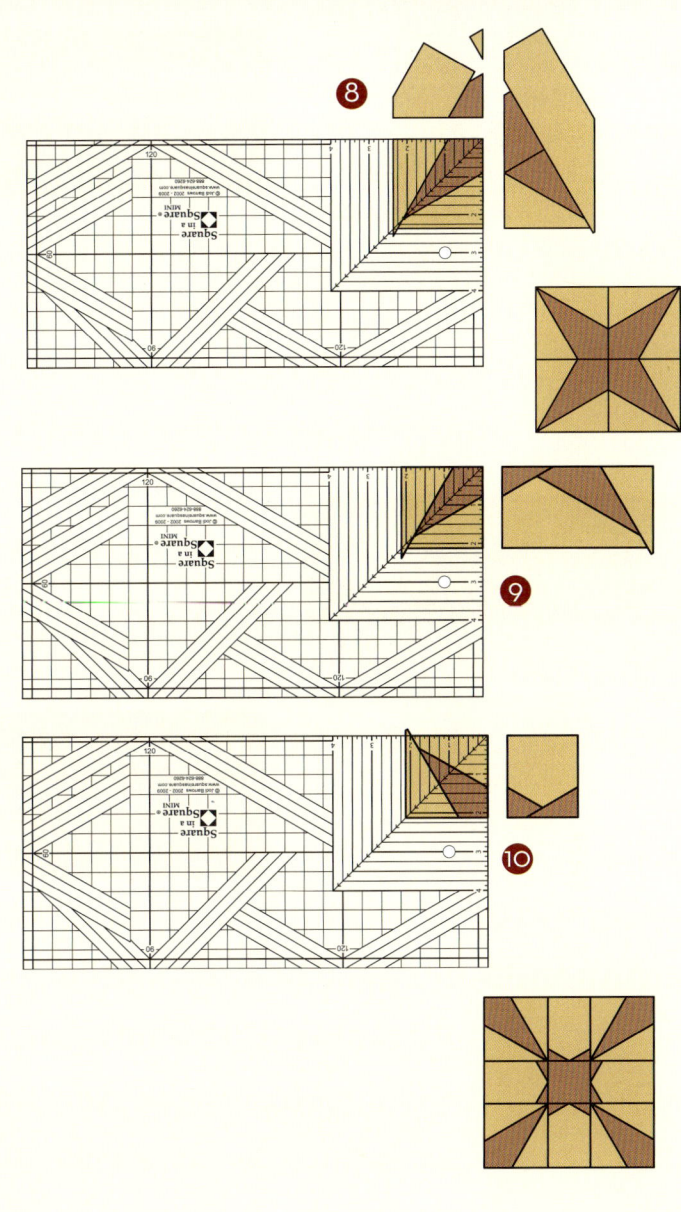

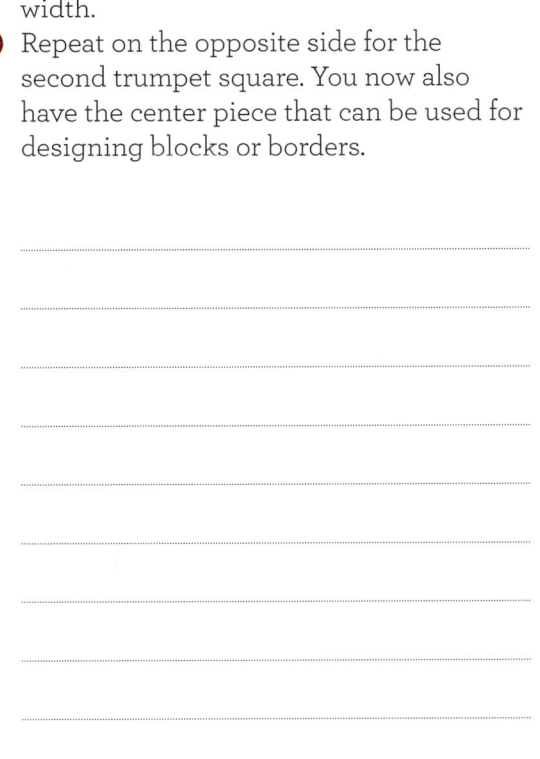

For additional help with the Option 39 Trumpet Square, visit **squareinasquare.com** *for a step-by-step instructional video.*

Option Sizing

The following Option sizing charts list the cut center square and cut strip sizes for each of the Square in a Square® Options for various sewn (finished) sizes. When figuring sizes for any quilt design, remember there are two sizes to work with. The smaller size is the sewn (finished) or graph paper size. The larger size is the cut (unfinished) or raw size. Always make sure you are working with the correct size.

Option 1
Instructions on page 16.

Sewn (finished) Size	Cut Center Square	Cut Strip Size
1	1 ¼	¾
1 ¼	1 ⅜	1
1 ½	1 ⅝	1 ⅛
1 ¾	1 ¾	1 ¼
2	2	1 ¼
2 ¼	2 ⅛	1 ⅜
2 ½	2 ¼	1 ⅜
2 ¾	2 ½	1 ½
3	2 ⅝	1 ⅝
3 ¼	2 ¾	1 ⅝
3 ½	3	1 ¾
3 ¾	3 ⅛	1 ⅞
4	3 ⅜	1 ⅞
4 ¼	3 ½	2
4 ½	3 ⅝	2 ⅛
4 ¾	3 ⅞	2 ¼
5	4	2 ½
6	4 ¾	2 ¾
8	6 ⅛	3 ½
10	7 ½	4 ¼
12	8 ½	4 ¾

Option 3
Flying Geese
Instructions on page 18.

Sewn (finished) Size	Cut Center Square	Cut Strip Size
1 x 2	2 ¼	1 ⅜
1 ¼ x 2 ½	2 ⅝	1 ⅝
1 ½ x 3	3	1 ¾
1 ¾ x 3 ½	3 ⅜	2
2 x 4	3 ¾	2 ⅛
2 ¼ x 4 ½	4	2 ¼
2 ½ x 5	4 ⅜	2 ½
2 ¾ x 5 ½	4 ¾	2 ⅝
3 x 6	5 ⅛	2 ⅞

Option 7
Basic Diamond
Instructions on page 20.

Sewn (finished) Size	Cut Center Diamond	Cut Strip Size
1 x 1 ¾	1 ⅜	1
1 ¼ x 2	1 ½	1
1 ½ x 2 ½	1 ¾	1 ⅛
1 ¾ x 3	2	1 ¼
2 x 3 ½	2 ¼	1 ⅜
2 ¼ x 4	2 ½	1 ½
2 ½ x 4 ¼	2 ¾	1 ⅝
2 ¾ x 4 ⅝	2 ⅞	1 ¾
3 x 5 ¼	3 ¼	1 ⅞
3 ¼ x 5 ¾	3 ⅜	2
3 ½ x 6 ¼	3 ½	2
3 ¾ x 6 ⅝	3 ¾	2 ⅛
4 x 7	4	2 ¼
4 ¼ x 7 ½	4 ¼	2 ⅜

Option 4
Half Square Triangles
Instructions on page 19.

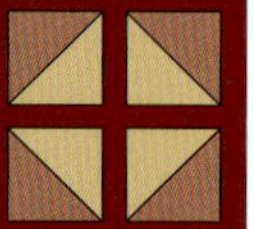

Sewn (finished) Size	Cut Center Square	Cut Strip Size
½	2	1 ¼
1	2 ⅝	1 ½
1 ¼	3	1 ¾
1 ½	3 ⅜	2
1 ¾	3 ⅝	2 ⅛
2	4	2 ¼
2 ¼	4 ⅜	2 ½
2 ½	4 ¾	2 ⅝
2 ¾	5	2 ¾
3	5 ½	3

Center Diamond Measurements
Diamonds per Strip
Based on a 40" strip, cut selvedge to selvedge

Strip Width	Number of Diamonds
2"	17
2 ½"	14
3"	9
3 ½"	9
4"	8
5"	7

Diamond Blocks Variations (cont.)

Canadian Geese Inverted		Canadian Geese Inverted		Canadian Geese Inverted		Canadian Geese Inverted	

Diamond Blocks Variations (cont.)

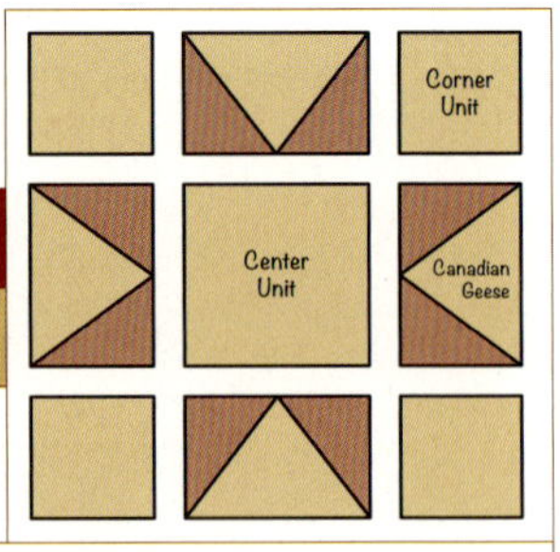

Block Size: 11 ½" cut, 11" sewn		
Corner Units		
	Solid Square	(1) 4" cut strip yields 2 blocks totaling (10) **corner squares**
	Option #4 Half Square	(1) 6 ⅛" cut strip yields 6 blocks totaling (6) **center squares for Option #4** (1) 3 ½" cut **surround strip** yields 2 blocks or (2) **Option #4s**
	4-Patch	(1) 2" cut strip of background yields 20 squares totaling (10) **4-Patch units** (1) 2" cut strip of color yields 20 squares totaling (10) **4-Patch units**
	Option #11	(1) 4 ½" cut strip yields 8 blocks totaling (8) **center squares for Option 11s** (1) 2 ½" cut row 1 **surround strip**, yields 3 blocks or (3) **Option 11s** (1) 3 ½" cut row 2 **surround strip** yields 2 blocks or (2) **Option 11s**
	Option #14	(1) 3 ⅝" cut strip yields 10 blocks totaling (10) **center squares for Option #14** (1) 2 ⅛" cut row 1 **surround strip** yields 3 blocks or (3) **Option 14s** (1) 3" cut row 2 **surround strip** yields 3 blocks or (3) **Option 14s** (1) 3 ¾" cut row 3 **surround strip** yields 2 blocks or (2) **Option 14s**
Center Units		
	Solid Square	(1) 4 ½" cut strip yields 8 blocks totaling (8) **center units**
	Option #1	(1) 3 ⅜" cut strip yields 11 blocks totaling (11) center squares for **Option #1** (1) 1 ⅞" cut **surround strip** yields 3 blocks or (3) **Option #1s**
	4-Patch	(1) 2 ½" cut strip of background yields 16 squares totaling (8) **4-Patch units** (1) 2 ½" cut strip of color yields 16 squares totaling (8) **4-Patch units**
	Option #4 Pinwheel	(1) 4" cut strip yields 10 blocks totaling (10) **center squares for Option #4s** (1) 2 ¼" **surround strip** yields 3 blocks or (3) **Option #4s**
Option #18		
	Canadian Geese	(1) 4 ¼" cut strip yields (10) **center diamonds** totaling (20) **Canadian Geese** (1) 2 ⅜" cut **surround strip** yields 3 diamond units totaling (6) **Canadian Geese**

Diamond Blocks Variations (cont.)

	Canadian Geese Inverted			Canadian Geese Inverted			Canadian Geese Inverted			Canadian Geese Inverted

Diamond Blocks Variations (cont.)

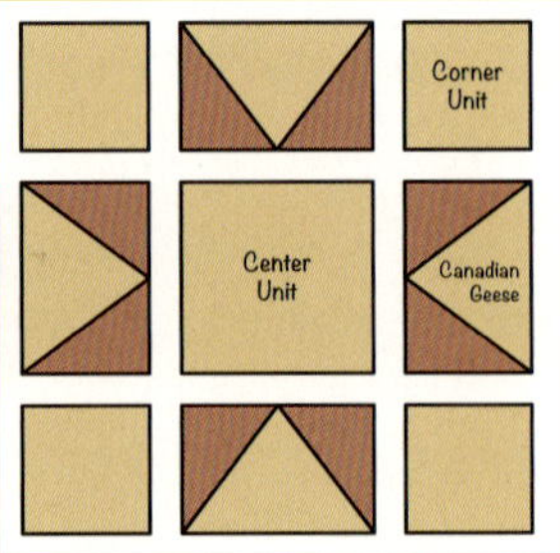

	Block Size:	10" cut, 9 ½" sewn
	Corner Units	
	Solid Square	(1) 3 ½" cut strip yields 2 blocks totaling (11) **corner squares**
	Option #4 Half Square	(1) 5 ½" cut strip yields 7 blocks totaling (7) **center squares for Option #4** (1) 3" cut **surround strip** yields 1.5 blocks or (1.5) **Option #4s**
	4-Patch	(1) 2" cut strip of background yields 20 squares totaling (10) **4-Patch units** (1) 2" cut strip of color yields 20 squares totaling (10) **4-Patch units**
	Option #11	(1) 4" cut strip yields 10 blocks totaling (10) **center squares for Option 11s** (1) 2 ¼" cut row 1 **surround strip**, yields 3 blocks or (3) **Option 11s** (1) 3 ¼" cut row 2 **surround strip** yields 2 blocks or (2) **Option 11s**
	Option #14	(1) 3 ⅜" cut strip yields 10 blocks totaling (10) **center squares for Option #14** (1) 2" cut row 1 **surround strip** yields 3 blocks or (3) **Option 14s** (1) 2 ½" cut row 2 **surround strip** yields 3 blocks or (3) **Option 14s** (1) 3 ½" cut row 3 **surround strip** yields 2 blocks or (2) **Option 14s**
	Center Units	
	Solid Square	(1) 4" cut strip yields 10 blocks totaling (10) **center units**
	Option #1	(1) 3" cut strip yields 13 blocks totaling (13) **center squares for Option #1** (1) 1 ¾" cut **surround strip** yields 3 blocks or (3) **Option #1s**
	4-Patch	(1) 2 ¼" cut strip of background yields 17 squares totaling (8.5) **4-Patch units** (1) 2 ¼" cut strip of color yields 17 squares totaling (8.5) **4-Patch units**
	Option #4 Pinwheel	(1) 3 ¾" cut strip yields 10 blocks totaling (10) **center squares for Option #4s** (1) 2 ⅛" **surround strip** yields 3 blocks or (3) **Option #4s**
	Option #18	
	Canadian Geese	(1) 2 ⅞" cut strip yields (13) **center diamonds** totaling (26) **Canadian Geese** (1) 1 ¾" cut **surround strip** yields 2 diamond units totaling (4) **Canadian Geese**

Diamond Blocks Variations (cont.)

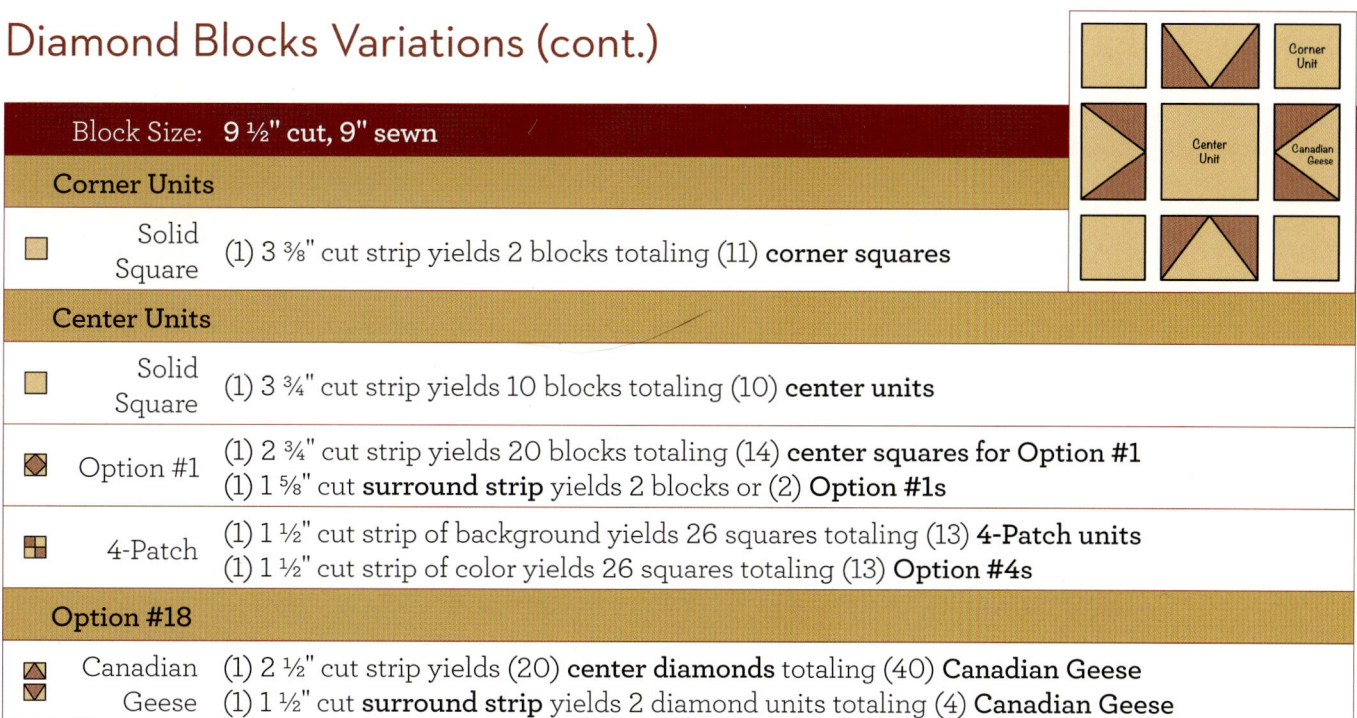

		Block Size: 9 ½" cut, 9" sewn
Corner Units		
☐	Solid Square	(1) 3 ⅜" cut strip yields 2 blocks totaling (11) **corner squares**
Center Units		
☐	Solid Square	(1) 3 ¾" cut strip yields 10 blocks totaling (10) **center units**
◆	Option #1	(1) 2 ¾" cut strip yields 20 blocks totaling (14) **center squares for Option #1** (1) 1 ⅝" cut **surround strip** yields 2 blocks or (2) **Option #1s**
▦	4-Patch	(1) 1 ½" cut strip of background yields 26 squares totaling (13) **4-Patch units** (1) 1 ½" cut strip of color yields 26 squares totaling (13) **Option #4s**
Option #18		
▲▼	Canadian Geese	(1) 2 ½" cut strip yields (20) **center diamonds** totaling (40) **Canadian Geese** (1) 1 ½" cut **surround strip** yields 2 diamond units totaling (4) **Canadian Geese**

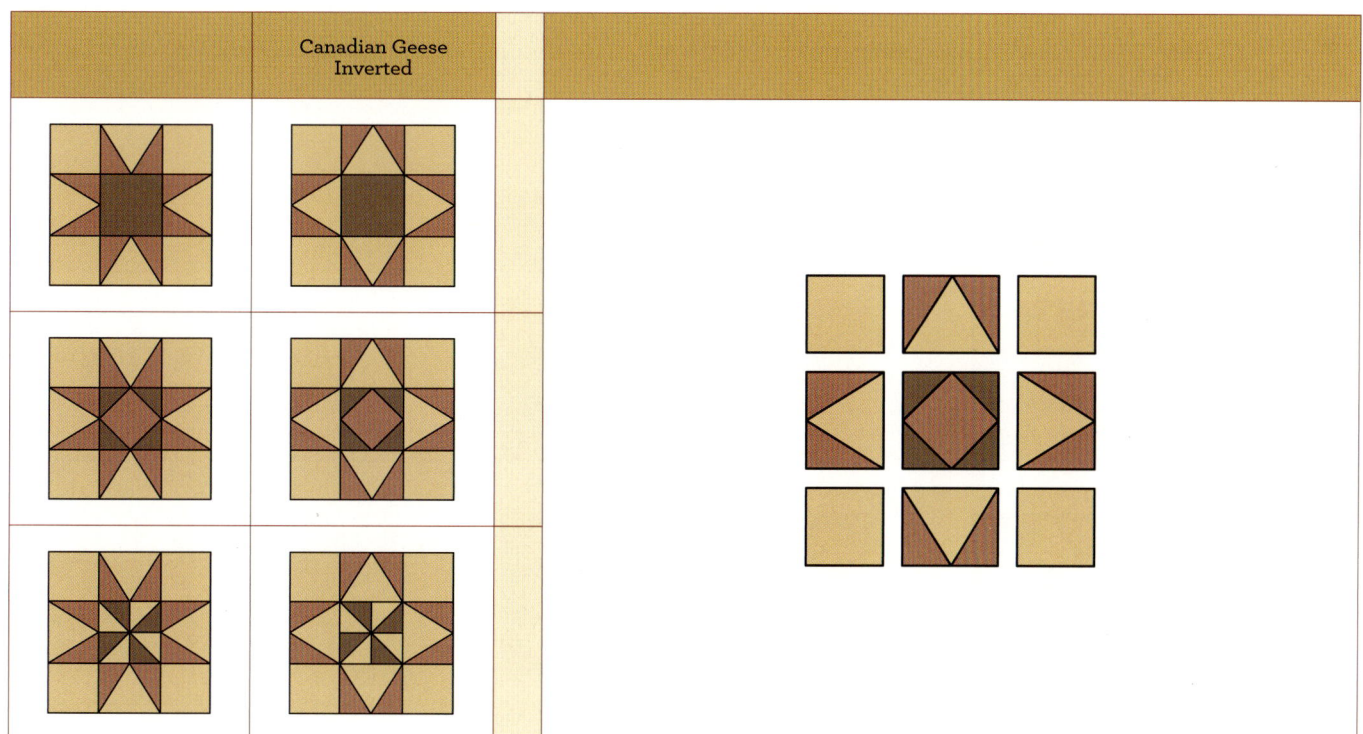

Diamond Blocks Variations (cont.)

Block Size:	8" cut, 7 ½" sewn	
Corner Units		
	Solid Square	(1) 2 ⅞" cut strip yields 3 blocks totaling (14) **corner squares**
	Option #4 Half Square	(1) 4 ⅝" cut strip yields 8 blocks totaling (8) **center squares for Option #4** (1) 2 ½" cut surround strip yields 2 blocks or (2) **Option #4s**
Center Units		
	Solid Square	(1) 3 ¼" cut strip yields 12 blocks totaling (12) **center units**
	Option #1	(1) 2 ½" cut strip yields 16 blocks totaling (16) **center squares for Option #1** (1) 1 ½" cut surround strip yields 4 blocks or (4) **Option #1s**
	Option #4 Pin-wheel	(1) 3 ½" cut strip yields 11 blocks totaling (11) **center squares for Option #4s** (1) 2" **surround strip** yields blocks or (2) **Option #4s**
Option #18		
	Canadian Geese	(1) 3½" cut strip yields (10) **center diamonds** totaling (20) **Canadian Geese** (1) 2" cut **surround strip** yields 2 diamond units totaling (4) **Canadian Geese**

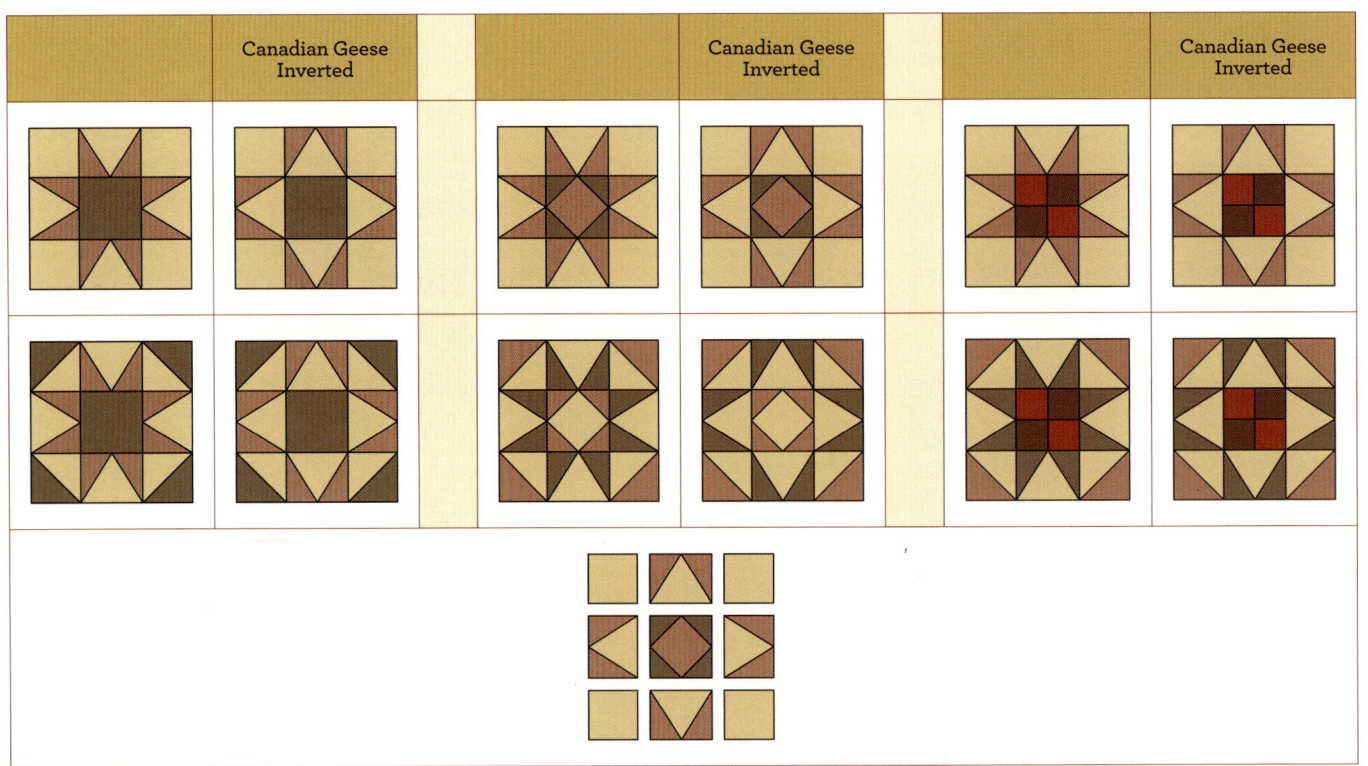

Diamond Blocks Variations (cont.)

	Canadian Geese Inverted		Canadian Geese Inverted		Canadian Geese Inverted		Canadian Geese Inverted

Diamond Blocks Variations (cont.)

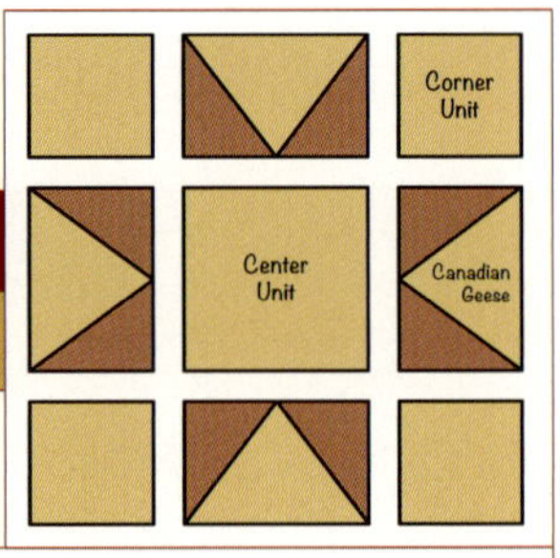

	Block Size:	7 ½" cut, 7" sewn
	Corner Units	
	Solid Square	(1) 2 ⅝" cut strip yields 3 blocks totaling (14) **corner squares**
	Option #4 Half Square	(1) 4 ⅜" cut strip yields 8 blocks totaling (8) **center squares for Option #4** (1) 2 ½" cut surround strip yields 2 blocks or (2) **Option #4s**
	4-Patch	(1) 1 ⅝" cut strip of background yields 22 squares totaling (11) **4-Patch units** (1) 1 ⅜" cut strip of color yields 22 squares totaling (11) **4-Patch units**
	Option #11	(1) 3 ¼" cut strip yields 12 blocks totaling (12) **center squares for Option 11s** (1) 1 ¾" cut row 1 surround strip, yields 3 blocks or (3) **Option 11s** (1) 2 ¼" cut row 2 surround strip yields 2 blocks or (2) **Option 11s**
	Option #14	(1) 2 ¾" cut strip yields 14 blocks totaling (14) **center squares for Option #14** (1) 1 ¾" cut row 1 surround strip yields 3 blocks or (3) **Option 14s** (1) 2 ¼" cut row 2 surround strip yields 2 blocks or (2) **Option 14s** (1) 3" cut row 3 surround strip yields 3 blocks or (3) **Option 14s**
	Center Units	
	Solid Square	(1) 3" cut strip yields 14 blocks totaling (14) **center units**
	Option #1	(1) 2 ¼" cut strip yields 17 blocks totaling (17) **center squares for Option #1** (1) 1 ⅜" cut surround strip yields 4 blocks or (4) **Option #1s**
	4-Patch	(1) 1 ¾" cut strip of background yields 22 squares totaling (11) **4-Patch units** (1) 1 ¾" cut strip of color yields 22 squares totaling (11) **4-Patch units**
	Option #4 Pinwheel	(1) 3" cut strip yields 13 blocks totaling (13) **center squares for Option #4s** (1) 1 ¾" surround strip yields 3 blocks or (3) **Option #4s**
	Option #18	
	Canadian Geese	(1) 2 ⅞" cut strip yields (13) **center diamonds** totaling (26) **Canadian Geese** (1) 1 ¾" cut surround strip yields 2 diamond units totaling (4) **Canadian Geese**

Diamond Blocks Variations (cont.)

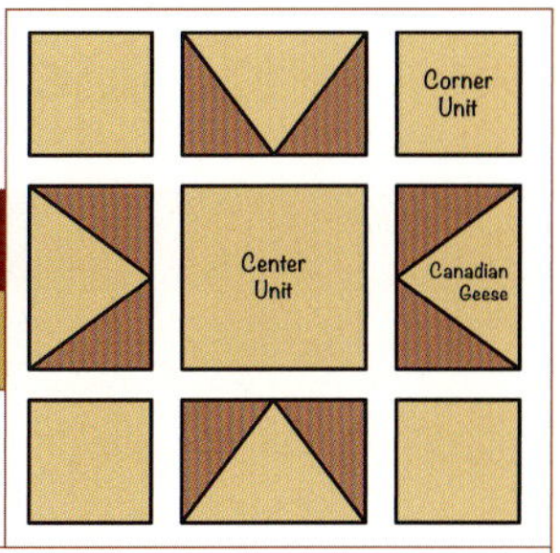

Block Size:	6" cut, 5 ½" sewn	
Corner Units		
	Solid Square	(1) 2 ¼" cut strip yields 4 blocks totaling (17) **corner squares**
	Option #4 Half Square	(1) 3 ⅝" cut strip yields 10 blocks totaling (10) **center squares for Option #4** (1) 2 ⅛" cut **surround strip** yields 2 blocks or (2) **Option #4s**
	4-Patch	(1) 1 ⅜" cut strip of background yields 26 squares totaling (13) **4-Patch units** (1) 1 ⅜" cut strip of color yields 26 squares totaling (13) **4-Patch units**
	Hour Glass	(1) 2 ½" cut strip yields 8 blocks totaling (32) **center squares for hour glass units** (1) 1 ½" cut **surround strip** yields 1 block or (10) **hour glass units** (1) 1 ⅜" cut strip yields 3 blocks totaling (26) **solid square units for hour glass units**
Center Units		
	Solid Square	(1) 2 ½" cut strip yields 16 blocks totaling (16) **center units**
	Option #1	(1) 2" cut strip yields 20 blocks totaling (20) **center squares for Option #1** (1) 1 ¼" cut surround strip yields 5 blocks or (5) **Option #1s**
	4-Patch	(1) 1 ½" cut strip of background yields 26 squares totaling (13) **4-Patch units** (1) 1 ½" cut strip of color yields 26 squares totaling (13) **4-Patch units**
Option #18		
	Canadian Geese	(1) 2 ½" cut strip yields (20) center diamonds totaling (40) **Canadian Geese** (1) 1 ½" cut surround strip yields 2 diamond units totaling (4) **Canadian Geese**

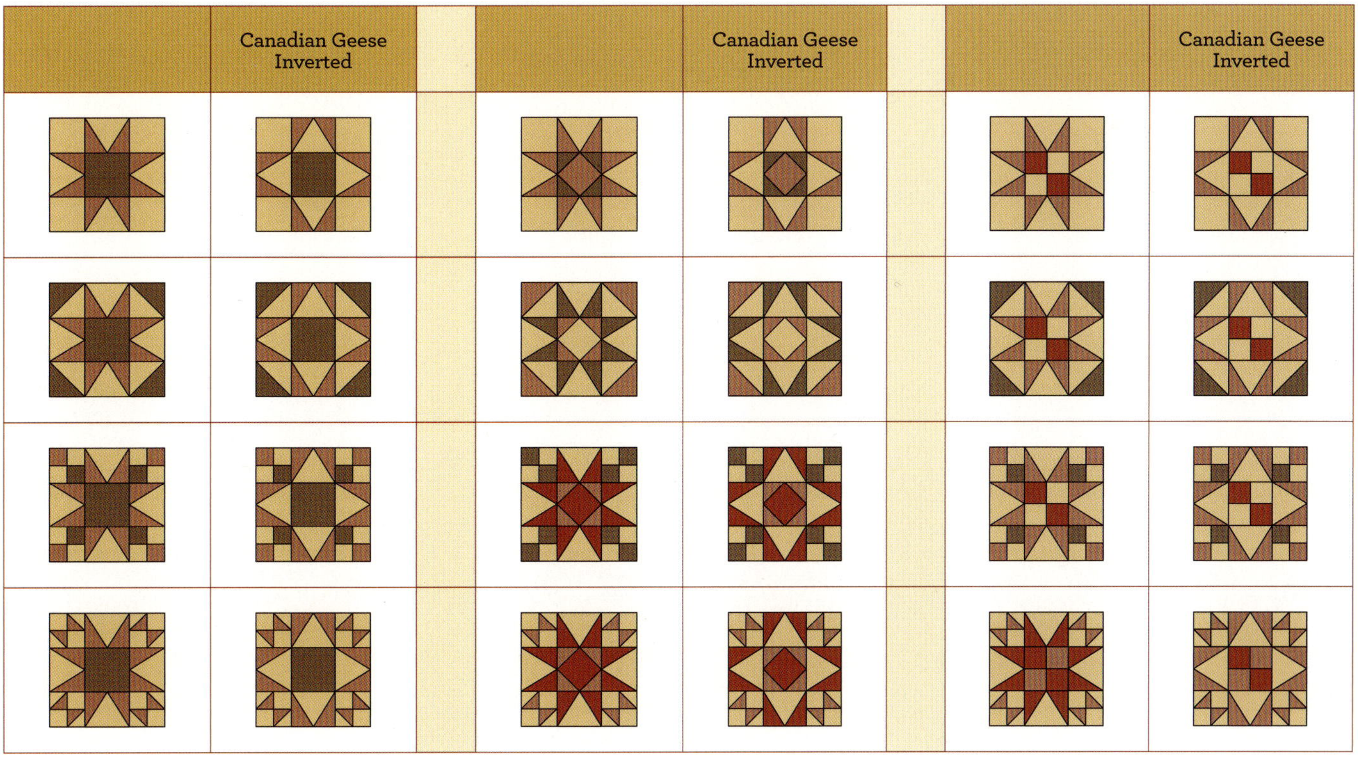

	Canadian Geese Inverted		Canadian Geese Inverted		Canadian Geese Inverted

76

Diamond Blocks Variations (cont.)

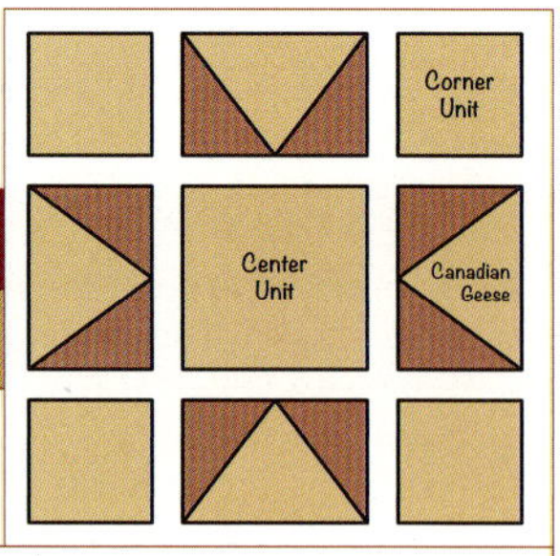

Block Size: 4 ½" cut, 4" sewn		
Corner Units		
☐	Solid Square	(1) 1 ¾" cut strip yields 5 blocks totaling (22) **corner squares**
◩	Option #4 Half Square	(1) 3" cut strip yields 13 blocks totaling (13) **center squares for Option #4** 1 ¾" cut **surround strip** yields 5 blocks or (5) **Option #4s**
⊞	4-Patch	(1) 1 ⅛" cut strip of background yields 32 squares totaling (16) **4-Patch units** (1) 1 ⅛" cut strip of color yields 32 squares totaling (16) **4-Patch units**
Center Units		
☐	Solid Square	(1) 2" cut strip yields 20 blocks totaling (20) **center units**
◆	Option #1	(1) 1 ⅝" cut strip yields 22 blocks totaling (22) **center squares for Option #1** (1) 1 ⅛" cut surround strip yields 5 blocks or (5) **Option #1s**
⊞	4-Patch	(1) 1 ¼" cut strip of background yields 40 squares totaling (20) **4-Patch units** 1 ¼" cut strip of color yields 40 squares totaling (20) **4-Patch units**
Option #18		
◮◭	Canadian Geese	(1) 2" cut strip yields (20) **center diamonds** totaling (40) **Canadian Geese** (1) 1 ¼" cut **surround strip** yields 4 diamond units totaling (8) **Canadian Geese**

75

Diamond Blocks Variations (cont.)

		Block Size: 3" cut, 2 ½" sewn
Corner Units		
▫	Solid Square	(1) 1 ¼" cut strip yields 8 blocks totaling (32) **corner squares**
◩	Option #4 Half Square	(1) 2 ¼" cut strip yields 17 blocks totaling (17) **center squares for Option #4** (1) 1 ½" cut surround strip yields 4 blocks or (4) **Option #4s**
Center Units		
▫	Solid Square	(1) 1 ½" cut strip yields 26 blocks totaling (26) **center units**
◆	Option #1	(1) 1 ¼" cut strip yields 32 blocks totaling (32) **center squares for Option #1** (1) ¾" cut surround strip yields 5 blocks or (5) **Option #1s**
⊞	4-Patch	(1) 1" cut strip of background yields 40 squares totaling (20) **4-Patch units** (1) 1" cut strip of color yields 40 squares totaling (20) **4-Patch units**
Option #18		
▲▽	Canadian Geese	(1) 1 ½" cut strip yields (20) **center diamonds** totaling (40) **Canadian Geese** (1) 1" cut surround strip yields 5 diamond units totaling (10) **Canadian Geese**

Canadian Geese Inverted   Canadian Geese Inverted   Canadian Geese Inverted

Diamond Blocks Variations

Block Size:	2 ½" cut, 2" sewn
Corner Units	
Solid Square	(1) 1 ⅛" cut strip yields 9 blocks totaling (36) **corner squares**
Option #4 Half Square	(1) 2 ⅛" cut strip yields 18 blocks totaling (18) **center squares for Option #4** (1) 1 ¼" cut surround strip yields 4 blocks or (4) **Option #4s**
Center Units	
Solid Square	(1) 1 ¼" cut strip yields 32 blocks totaling (32) **center units**
4-Patch	(1) ⅞" cut strip of background yields 40 squares totaling (20) **4-Patch units** (1) ⅞" cut strip of color yields 40 squares totaling (20) **4-Patch units**
Option #18	
Canadian Geese	(1) 1 ⅜" cut strip yields (20) **center diamonds** totaling (40) **Canadian Geese** (1) 1" cut **surround strip** yields 5 diamond units totaling (10) **Canadian Geese**

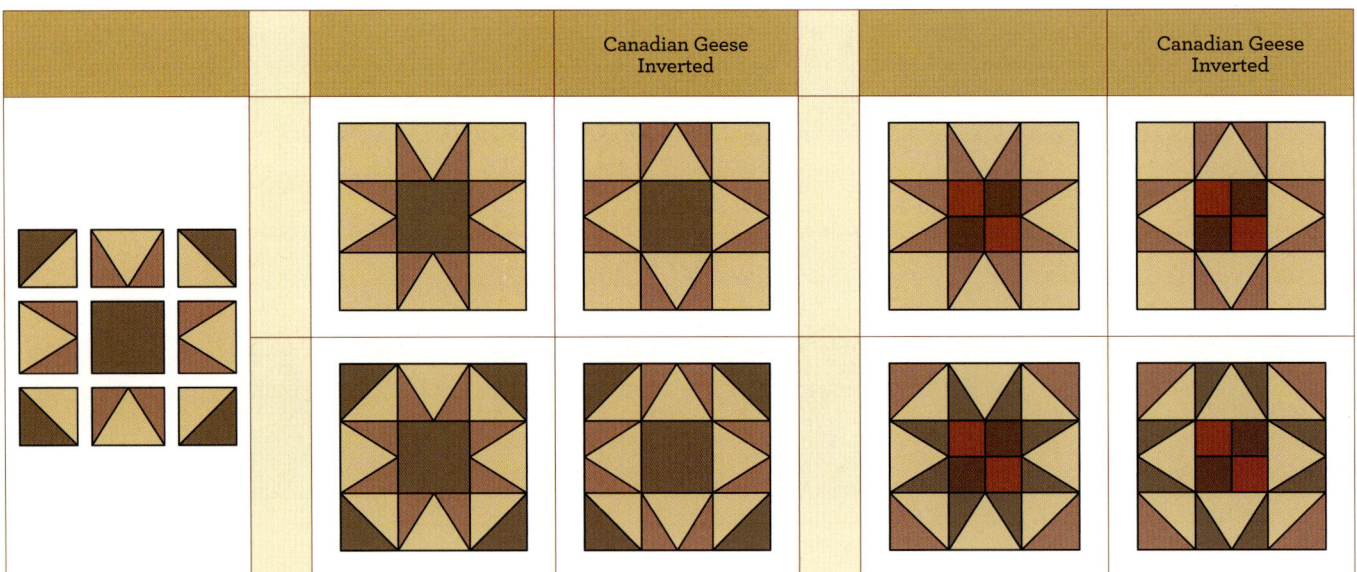

Block Building

Each star combination has four corner squares and center units that may be switched around. The center units chosen for the basic star are: a solid square, an Option #1, and Option #4 pinwheels, 4-Patch or 9-Patch center units. The corner squares may be solid units, 4-Patch, 9-Patch, Option #4 half square triangle units, Option #11 with mirrored units, Option #14 with mirrored units, or an Option #4 half-square hourglass. The overall block may vary in size.

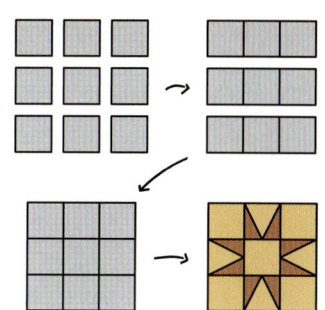

The star block with long thin triangle units was originally named "54-40 or Fight" This was named for the boundary lines in a war. Traditionally, the block was a 9-Patch block. This means 9 equal squares, 3 across, in 3 rows. The equal sized squares can have anything in them.

Using the Square in a Square® technique we achieve the same look, but we go about it a little differently. This system requires the 60° and 120° angles to create the long thin triangle units whereas traditional sizing used a tighter angle to keep each unit square. Our units will be slightly different but will have the same look.

Sewn and Cut Size of the Option #7 Unit

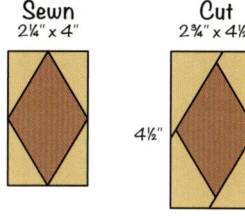

Cutting for the Diamond Unit (Option #18 – Canadian Geese) – north-south

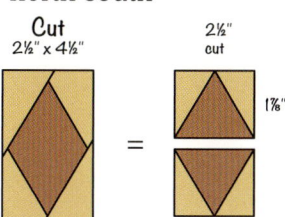

Notice the trimming is different for the Option #18 Canadian Geese compared to the Option #7. The trimming is different in order to move points and create seam allowances.

A 9-Patch is still used to create the block but not with the true squares. This example is with raw edge seam allowances or cut size.

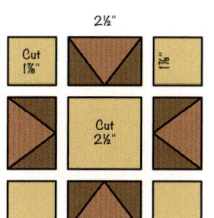

The Canadian Goose Option #18 unit is a cut, raw edge 2 ½" x 1 ⅞".

The corner units will be a cut 1 ⅞" square which is now the short side of the triangle unit. (east-west)

The center unit will be a cut 2 ½" square. The flat side of the triangles touching is the larger measurement and must match the center unit. (north-south)

The flat or short side (north-south) of the triangle unit is now the largest side of the #18 unit.

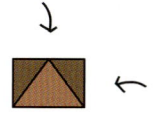

The long side (east-west) of the triangle unit is now the short side of the #18 unit.

This creates the look and is put together as a 9-Patch unit block. This is much easier than traditional piecing.

Option #18 Canadian Geese North Side Matching to a Solid Square
Option #1 | Option #3 | 4-Patch | Pinwheel

Row	 Sewn, Finish or Graph Paper N-S Side x E-W side	Cut Diamond Strip Size	Cut Surround Strip Size	 Cut Solid Square	 Option #1 Cut Center Square	Option #1 Cut Surround Strip Size	 Option #3 Cut Center Square	Option #3 Cut Surround Strip Size	 4-Patch Cut Strip Size	 Pinwheel Option #4 Cut Center Square	Pinwheel Option #4 Cut Surround Strip Size
1	¾ x ⅝	1 ⅜	1	1 ¼	1	¾	1 ⅜	¾	⅞	1 ¾	1
2	1 x ¾	1 ½	1	1 ½	1 ¼	¾	1 ⅝	1	1	2	1 ¼
3	1 ¼ x 1	1 ¾	1 ⅛	1 ¾	1 ⅜	1	1 ¾	1 ¼	1 ⅛	2 ⅛	1 ¼
4	1 ½ x 1 ¼	2	1 ¼	2	1 ⅝	1 ⅛	2	1 ¼	1 ¼	2 ¼	1 ¼
5	1 ¾ x 1 ½	2 ¼	1 ⅜	2 ¼	1 ¾	1 ¼	2 ⅛	1 ¼	1 ⅜	2 ½	1 ¼
6	2 x 1 ¾	2 ½	1 ½	2 ½	2	1 ¼	2 ⅜	1 ⅜	1 ½	2 ⅝	1 ½
7	2 ¼ x 2	2 ¾	1 ⅝	2 ¾	2 ⅛	1 ⅜	2 ½	1 ½	1 ⅝	2 ¾	1 ½
8	2 ½ x 2 ¼	2 ⅞	1 ¾	3	2 ¼	1 ⅜	2 ⅝	1 ⅝	1 ¾	3	1 ¾
9	2 ¾ x 2 ⅜	3 ¼	1 ⅞	3 ¼	2 ½	1 ½	2 ⅞	1 ¾	1 ⅞	3 ¼	1 ¾
10	3 x 2 ⅝	3 ⅜	2	3 ½	2 ⅝	1 ⅝	3	1 ¾	2	3 ⅜	2
11	3 ¼ x 2 ⅞	3 ½	2	3 ¾	2 ¾	1 ⅝	3 ⅛	1 ¾	2 ⅛	3 ½	2
12	3 ½ x 3	3 ¾	2 ⅛	4	3	1 ¾	3 ⅜	2	2 ¼	3 ⅝	2 ⅛
13	3 ¾ x 3 ¼	4	2 ¼	4 ¼	3 ⅛	1 ⅞	3 ½	2	2 ⅜	3 ⅞	2 ¼
14	4 x 3 ½	4 ¼	2 ⅜	4 ½	3 ⅜	1 ⅞	3 ¾	2 ⅛	2 ½	4	2 ¼

Center Diamond Measurements

Diamonds per Strip
(based on a 40" strip, cut selvedge to selvedge)

Strip Width	Number of Diamonds
2"	17
2 ½"	14
3"	9
3 ½"	9
4"	8
5"	7

Horizontal and Vertical Option #7 Chart
Matching to Canadian Geese – Option #18

Option #18 North End of Canadian Geese Matching to Short Side of Option #7 Rectangle

Option #18 North End of Canadian Geese Matching to Long Side of Option #7 Rectangle

Row	Cut Strip for Center Diamond	Cut Size Surround Strip	Cut Strip for Center Diamond	Cut Size Surround Strip
1	1 ½	1	2 ¼	1 ⅜
2	1 ¾	1 ⅛	2 ½	1 ½
3	2	1 ¼	2 ⅞	1 ¾
4	2 ¼	1 ⅜	3 ⅜	2
5	2 ½	1 ½	3 ¾	2 ⅛
6	2 ¾	1 ⅝	4 ¼	2 ⅜
7	2 ⅞	1 ¾		
8	3 ¼	1 ⅞		
9	3 ⅜	2		
10	3 ½	2		
11	3 ¾	2 ⅛		
12	4	2 ¼		
13	4 ¼	2 ⅜		

Option #7 Chart Matching to Option #4 or a Pinwheel

Refer to Option #7 diamond measurements. Follow the row number from any of these charts. Multiple units all match to create your design.

	Option #4 Half Square Triangle Matching to Short Side of Rectangle Unit		Pinwheel Option #4 Matching to Short Side of Rectangle Unit			Pinwheel Option #4 Matching to Long Side of Rectangle Unit		
			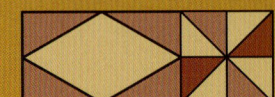					
Row	Cut Center Square	Cut Strip Size	Cut Center Square	Cut Strip Size	Pinwheel Sewn, Finished or Graph Paper Size	Cut Center Square	Cut Strip Size	Pinwheel Sewn, Finished or Graph Paper Size
1	2 ⅝	1 ½	2	1 ¼	1	2 ½	1 ½	1 ¾
2	3	1 ¾	2 ⅛	1 ⅜	1 ¼	2 ¾	1 ⅝	2
3	3 ⅜	2	2 ⅜	1 ½	1 ½	3	1 ¾	2 ½
4	3 ⅝	2 ⅛	2 ½	1 ½	1 ¾	3 ⅜	2	3
5	4	2 ¼	2 ¾	1 ⅝	2	3 ¾	2 ⅛	3 ½
6	4 ⅜	2 ½	2 ⅞	1 ¾	2 ¼	4 ⅛	2 ⅜	4
7	4 ¾	2 ⅝	3	1 ¾	2 ½	4 ¼	2 ⅜	4 ¼
8	5	2 ¾	3 ¼	1 ⅞	2 ¾	4 ⅝	2 ⅝	4 ⅝
9	5 ½	3 ¼	3 ⅜	2	3	4 ⅞	2 ¾	5 ¼
10	5 ⅞	3 ½	3 ½	2	3 ¼	5 ¼	2 ⅞	5 ¾
11	6 ⅛	3 ⅝	3 ⅝	2 ⅛	3 ½	6	3 ¼	6 ¾
12	6 ½	3 ¾	3 ⅞	2 ¼	3 ¾	6 ⅛	3 ½	7 ⅛
13	6 ⅞	4	4 ⅛	2 ⅜	4	6 ½	3 ¾	7 ½
14	7 ¼	4 ¼	4 ¼	2 ⅜	4 ¼	6 ⅞	4	8

Option #7 Chart Matching to 4-Patch

Refer to Option #7 diamond measurements. Follow the row number from any of these charts. Multiple units all match to create your design.

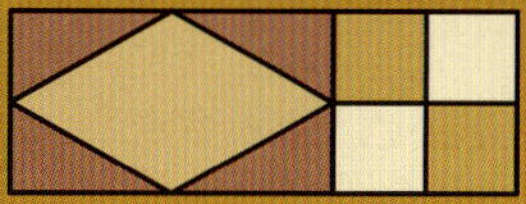

Row	4-Patch Matching to Short Side of Option #7 Rectangle 4-Patch Cut Strip Size	4-Patch Matching to Long Side of Option #7 Rectangle 4-Patch Cut Strip Size
1	1	1 ⅜
2	1 ⅛	1 ½
3	1 ¼	1 ¾
4	1 ⅜	2
5	1 ½	2 ¼
6	1 ⅝	2 ½
7	1 ¾	2 ⅝
8	1 ⅞	2 ⅞
9	2	3 ⅛
10	2 ⅛	3 ⅝
11	2 ¼	3 ⅞
12	2 ⅜	4 ⅛
13	2 ½	4 ¼
14	2 ⅝	4 ½

Diamond Charts

Option #7 Charts Matching to Desired Units

There are 14 rows on this chart. Follow any corresponding row on the chart and the units will match up to create units or blocks. For example, use any measurements on row 2 and they will sew together to create a beautiful quilt block design. Watch the top diagrams to find the unit required. Next, read the top of the column to find the cut size. All designs start from scratch with graph paper. **Remember, sewn-finished and graph paper are all the same measurements or size.** For this book we want to know what would match up to the Option #7 and #18. Also, if the units have a horizontal or vertical side to match. You may need to refer to Opton #7 **Basic Diamond** cutting and sewing. On the next several pages you have many charts showing units "matching to" each other. Remember, each row corresponds to a chart on the next few pages.

Option #7 Chart
Follow the row number to match up with any of the other charts

Row	 Rectangle Graph Paper Measurement	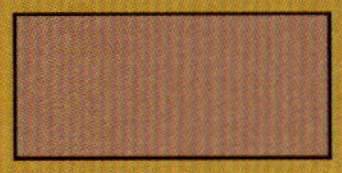 Cut Rectangle Size	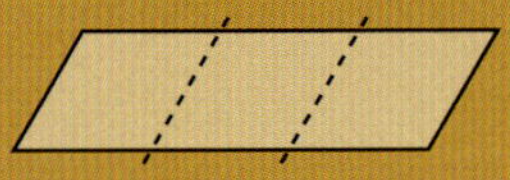 Cut Strip for #7 Center Diamond	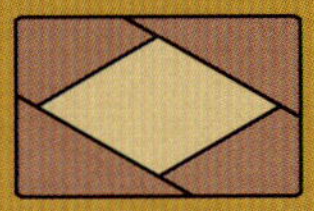 Cut #7 Surround Strip
1	1 x 1 ¾	1 ½ x 2 ¼	1 ⅜	1
2	1 ¼ x 2	1 ¾ x 2 ½	1 ½	1
3	1 ½ x 2 ½	2 x 3	1 ¾	1 ⅛
4	1 ¾ x 3	2 ¼ x 3 ½	2	1 ¼
5	2 x 3 ½	2 ½ x 4	2 ¼	1 ⅜
6	2 ¼ x 4	2 ¾ x 4 ½	2 ½	1 ½
7	2 ½ x 4 ¼	3 x 4 ¾	2 ¾	1 ⅝
8	2 ¾ x 4 ⅝	3 ¼ x 5 ⅛	2 ⅞	1 ¾
9	3 x 5 ¼	3 ½ x 5 ¾	3 ¼	1 ⅞
10	3 ¼ x 5 ¾	3 ¾ x 6 ¼	3 ⅜	2
11	3 ½ x 6 ¼	4 x 6 ¾	3 ½	2
12	3 ¾ x 6 ⅝	4 ¼ x 7 ⅛	3 ¾	2 ⅛
13	4 x 7	4 ½ x 7 ½	4	2 ¼
14	4 ¼ x 7 ½	4 ¾ x 8	4 ¼	2 ⅜

Option 38

Instructions on page 46.

Cut Size of Rectangle Unit	Sewn Size of Rectangle Unit	Cut Size of Center Diamond Strip	Cut Size of Surround Strip for Row 1	Cut Size of Surround Strip for Row 2	Cut Size of Surround Strip for Row 3	Sewn Size with Row 2	Cut Size with Row 2
2 ⅛	1 ⅞	1 ½	1	1 ¼	1 ½	1 ⅛	1 ⅝
2 ¼	1 ¾	1 ⅝	1	1 ¼	1 ½	1 ¼	1 ¾
2 ⅞	2 ⅜	1 ¾	1 ⅛	1 ¼	1 ½	1 ⅝	2 ⅛
3	2 ½	1 ⅞	1 ¼	1 ¼	1 ½	1 ¾	2 ¼
3 ½	3	2	1 ¼	1 ½	1 ¾	2	2 ½
3 ¾	3 ¼	2 ⅛	1 ¼	1 ½	1 ¾	2 ⅜	2 ⅞
4	3 ½	2 ¼	1 ⅜	1 ½	2	2 ½	3
4 ¾	4 ¼	2 ⅜	1 ½	1 ½	2	3	3 ½
5	4 ½	2 ½	1 ½	1 ¼ + 1 ½	2 ⅛	3 ¼	3 ¾
5 ½	5	2 ⅝	1 ½	1 ¼ + 1 ¾	2 ¼	3 ½	4
5 ¾	5 ¼	2 ¾	1 ⅝	1 ¼ + 1 ¾	2 ½	3 ¾	4 ¼
6	5 ½	2 ⅞	1 ¾	1 ½ + 2	2 ½	3 ⅞	4 ⅜
6 ¼	5 ¾	3	1 ¾	1 ½ + 2	2 ½	4	4 ½
7	6 ½	3 ⅛	1 ¾	1 ¾ + 2 ¼	3	4 ½	5
7 ½	7	3 ¼	1 ⅞	1 ¾ + 2 ½	3	5	5 ½
7 ¾	7 ¼	3 ⅜	2	2 + 2 ½	3 ¼	5 ⅜	5 ¾
8	7 ½	3 ½	2	2 + 2 ¾	3 ¼	5 ¼	5 ⅞
8 ½	8	3 ⅝	2 ⅛	2 + 2 ¾	3 ½	5 ⅜	6 ¼
9 ¼	8 ¾	3 ¾	2 ⅛	2 ¼ + 3	3 ½	6	6 ½
9 ½	9	3 ⅞	2 ¼	2 ¼ + 3 ¼	3 ½	6 ⅛	6 ⅝
9 ¾	9 ¼	4	2 ¼	2 ¼ + 3 ¼	3 ½	6 ½	7

Option 37
Granny Goose
Instructions on page 45.

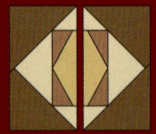

Cut Size of Rectangle Unit	Sewn Size of Rectangle Unit	Cut size of Center Diamond Strip	Cut size of Surround Strip for Row 1	Cut size of Surround Strip for Row 2	Cut size of Surround Strip for Row 3
2 ⅛ x 1 ⅛	1 ⅝ x ⅝	1 ½	1	1	1 ¼
2 ½ x 1 ½	2 x 1	1 ⅝	1	1 ¼	1 ½
2 ⅞ x 1 ¾	2 ⅜ x 1 ½	1 ¾	1 ⅛	1 ¼	1 ½
3 ⅜ x 2	2 ⅞ x 1 ½	1 ⅞	1 ¼	1 ½	1 ½
3 ⅝ x 2	3 ⅛ x 1 ½	2	1 ¼	1 ½	1 ¾
3 ⅞ x 2 ¼	3 ⅜ x 1 ¾	2 ⅛	1 ¼	1 ½	1 ¾
4 ⅜ x 2 ⅜	3 ⅞ x 1 ⅞	2 ¼	1 ⅜	1 ½ + 2	2
5 x 2 ¾	4 ½ x 2 ¼	2 ⅜	1 ½	1 ½ + 2	2 ¼
5 ¼ x 2 ⅞	4 ¾ x 2 ⅜	2 ½	1 ½	1 ½ + 2	2 ¼
5 ⅝ x 3 ⅛	5 ⅛ x 2 ⅝	2 ⅝	1 ½	1 ¾ + 2	2 ½
6 ¼ x 3 ⅜	5 ¾ x 2 ⅝	2 ¾	1 ⅝	1 ½ + 2 ¼	2 ¾
6 ⅜ x 3 ⅜	5 ⅞ x 2 ⅞	2 ⅞	1 ¾	1 ½ + 2 ¼	2 ¾
6 ½ x 3 ½	6 x 3	3	1 ¾	2 + 2 ¼	3
7 x 3 ¾	6 ½ x 3 ¼	3 ⅛	1 ¾	2 + 2 ½	3
7 ½ x 4	7 x 3 ½	3 ¼	1 ⅞	2 + 2 ½	3
8 x 4 ¼	7 ½ x 3 ¾	3 ⅜	2	2 + 2 ¾	3 ¼
8 x 4 ⅜	7 ½ x 3 ⅞	3 ½	2	2 ¼ + 3 ¼	3 ¼
8 ¾ x 4 ⅝	8 ¼ x 4 ⅛	3 ⅝	2 ⅛	2 ¼ + 3 ¼	3 ½
9 ⅛ x 4 ¾	8 ⅝ x 4 ¼	3 ¾	2 ⅛	2 ½ + 3 ¼	3 ¾
9 ½ x 5	9 x 4 ½	3 ⅞	2 ½	2 ½ + 3 ¼	4
9 ⅞ x 5 ⅛	9 ⅜ x 4 ⅝	4	2 ½	2 ½ + 3 ½	4 ½

Option 36

Rooftop Triangle

Instructions on page 44.

Sewn Inside Angle	Cut Size of Center Diamond Strip	Cut Size of Surround Strip for Row 1	Cut Size of Surround Strip for Row 2	Sewn size of individual Option 36 Triangle Unit
1 ⅞	1 ⅜	1	1	1 ⅜ x 1 ⅛
2 ⅛	1 ½	1	1	1 ⅝ x 1 ⅜
2 ½	1 ⅝	1	1	2 x 1 ⅜
3	1 ¾	1 ⅛	1 ¼	2 ½ x 1 ¾
3 ¼	1 ⅞	1 ¼	1 ¼	2 ¾ x 1 ⅞
3 ⅝	2	1 ¼	1 ½	3 ⅛ x 2 ¼
4	2 ⅛	1 ¼	1 ¾	3 ½ x 2 ⅜
4 ⅜	2 ¼	1 ⅜	1 ¾	3 ⅞ x 2 ⅞
4 ¾	2 ⅜	1 ½	1 ¾	4 ¼ x 3
5 ⅜	2 ½	1 ½	2	4 ⅞ x 3 ½
5 ⅝	2 ⅝	1 ½	2 ¼	5 ⅛ x 3 ⅝
5 ⅞	2 ¾	1 ⅝	2 ¼	5 ½ x 3 ⅞
6 ⅜	2 ⅞	1 ¾	2 ½	5 ⅞ x 4 ⅛
6 ½	3	1 ¾	2 ½	6 x 4 ⅜
6 ⅞	3 ⅛	1 ⅞	2 ½	6 ⅜ x 4 ⅝
7 ½	3 ¼	1 ⅞	2 ¾	7 x 5
7 ¾	3 ⅜	2	2 ¼ + 3	7 ¼ x 5 ⅛
9 ⅛	3 ½	2	2 ¼ + 3	8 ¼ x 5 ⅞
9 ½	3 ⅝	2	2 ¼ + 3 ¼	8 ⅝ x 6 ⅛
9 ⅞	3 ¾	2 ⅛	2 ¼ + 3 ¼	9 x 6 ⅜
10 ⅜	3 ⅞	2 ¼	2 ½ + 3 ½	9 ½ x 6 ⅞
10 ¾	4	2 ¼	2 ½ + 3 ½	9 ⅞ x 7

Option 35
Jodi's Favorite Corner Unit
Instructions on page 43.

Cut Size for Center Diamond	Cut Size Surround Strip Row 1	Cut Size Surround Strip Row 2	Unit Cut Size 2nd Round	Cut Size Surround Strip Row 3	Unit Cut Size 3rd Round
1 ½	1	¾	1	⅞	⅜
1 ⅝	1 ⅛	¾	1	1	½
1 ¾	1 ¼	1	1 ¼	1 ⅜	⅞
1 ⅞	1 ¼	1 ¼	1 ½	1 ½	1
2	1 ¼	1 ¼	1 ½	1 ¾	1 ¼
2 ⅛	1 ¼	1 ¼	1 ¾	1 ⅞	1 ⅜
2 ¼	1 ⅜	1 ½	2	2 ⅛	1 ⅝
2 ⅜	1 ½	1 ½	2	2 ¼	1 ¾
2 ½	1 ½	1 ¼ + 1 ½	2	2 ½	2
2 ⅝	1 ½	1 ¼ + 1 ¾	2 ¼	2 ¾	2 ¼
2 ¾	1 ⅝	1 ¼ + 1 ¾	2 ¼	2 ⅞	2 ⅜
2 ⅞	1 ¾	1 ½ + 2	2 ½	3	2 ½
3	1 ¾	1 ½ + 2	2 ½	3 ¼	2 ¾
3 ⅛	1 ¾	1 ¾ + 2 ¼	2 ¾	3 ⅜	2 ⅞
3 ¼	1 ⅞	1 ¾ + 2 ½	3	3 ⅝	3 ⅛
3 ⅜	2	2 + 2 ½	3	3 ¾	3 ¼
3 ½	2	2 + 2 ¾	3 ¼	3 ⅞	3 ⅜
3 ⅝	2 ⅛	2 + 2 ¾	3 ½	4 ¼	3 ¾
3 ¾	2 ⅛	2 ¼ + 3	3 ½	4 ½	4
3 ⅞	2 ¼	2 ¼ + 3 ¼	3 ½	4 ⅝	4 ¼
4	2 ¼	2 ¼ + 3 ¼	3 ¾	4 ⅞	4 ⅜
4 ⅛	2 ⅜	2 ¼ x 3 ½	4	5	4 ½

Option 33
The Snowball Block
Instructions on page 41.

Cut Size for Center Diamond	Cut Size of Surround Strip Row 1	Cut Size Snowball Unit	Sewn Size of Snowball
1 ⅜	1	1 ¼	¾
1 ½	1	1 ⅜	⅞
1 ⅝	1 ⅛	1 ⅜ x 1 ⅝	⅞ x 1 ¼
1 ¾	1 ¼	1 ⅝ x 2	1 ⅛ x 1 ½
1 ⅞	1 ¼	1 ¾ x 2 ⅛	1 ¼ x 1 ⅝
2	1 ¼	2 x 2 ½	1 ½ x 2
2 ⅛	1 ¼	2 ⅛ x 2 ⅝	1 ⅝ x 2 ¼
2 ¼	1 ⅜	2 ¼ x 2 ⅞	1 ¾ x 2 ⅜
2 ⅜	1 ½	2 ⅜ x 3 ⅛	1 ⅞ x 2 ⅝
2 ½	1 ½	2 ½ x 3 ½	2 x 3
2 ⅝	1 ½	2 ¾ x 3 ¾	2 ¼ x 3 ¼
2 ¾	1 ⅝	2 ⅞ x 4	2 ⅜ x 3 ½
2 ⅞	1 ¾	3 x 4 ¼	2 ½ x 3 ¾
3	1 ¾	3 ⅛ x 4 ½	2 ⅝ x 4
3 ⅛	1 ¾	3 ¼ x 4 ¾	2 ¾ x 4 ¼
3 ¼	1 ⅞	3 ⅜ x 5	2 ⅞ x 4 ½
3 ⅜	2	3 ½ x 5 ¼	3 x 4 ¾
3 ½	2	3 ⅝ x 5 ⅞	3 ⅛ x 5 ⅜
3 ⅝	2	2 ⅞ x 6 ⅜	3 ⅜ x 5 ⅞
3 ¾	2 ⅛	4 x 6 ⅝	3 ½ x 6 ⅛
3 ⅞	2 ¼	4 ⅛ x 6 ¾	3 ⅝ x 6 ¼
4	2 ¼	4 ¼ x 7	3 ¾ x 6 ½

Hints:
- The diamond units can be unusual to work with. The charts are designed to help you with the sizing of the options. Your own personal sewing personality and sewing equipment can alter the sizing of your unit, as well as how you understand the system and use your ruler. If you need to alter the size, just go up or down the center diamond column.
- When figuring size from scratch for any design, use the sewn measurements. The larger number is where you cut the option apart. It becomes the outside edge in most designs.
- Sewn measurments are the original outside edge of the option.
- Surround strip width can always be cut wider for easy strip cutting.
- When figuring borders, use the sewn measurements.

Option 32
Slim Jim
Instructions on page 40.

Cut Size for Center Diamond	Cut Size Surround Strip Row 1	Cut Size Surround Strip Row 2	Unit Cut Size 2nd Round	Cut Size Surround Strip Row 3	Unit Cut Size 3rd Round
1 ⅜	1	1	1 ½	1 ¼	1 x 2
1 ½	1	1	1 ¾	1 ½	1 ¼ x 2 ¼
1 ⅝	1	1	2	1 ½	1 ⅜ x 2 ⅜
1 ¾	1 ⅛	1 ⅛	2 ⅛	1 ½	1 ⅝ x 3
1 ⅞	1 ¼	1 ¼	2 ¼	1 ½	1 ⅞ x 3 ¼
2	1 ¼	1 + 1 ½	2 ½	1 ¾	2 ⅛ x 3 ⅝
2 ⅛	1 ¼	1 + 1 ¾	2 ¾	2	2 ¼ x 4
2 ¼	1 ⅜	1 + 2	3 ⅛	2 ¼	2 ½ x 4 ½
2 ⅜	1 ½	1 + 2	3 ⅜	2 ¼	2 ⅝ x 4 ¾
2 ½	1 ½	1 ¼ + 2 ¼	3 ¾	2 ½	2 ⅞ x 5 ¼
2 ⅝	1 ½	1 ¼ + 2 ¼	4	2 ½	3 x 5 ⅝
2 ¾	1 ⅝	1 ¼ + 2 ¼	4 ¼	2 ¾	3 ⅜ x 6 ¼
2 ⅞	1 ¾	1 ½ + 2 ½	4 ½	2 ¾	3 ½ x 6 ½
3	1 ¾	1 ½ + 2 ½	4 ¾	3	3 ¾ x 6 ¾
3 ⅛	1 ¾	1 ½ + 2 ¾	5	3 ¼	3 ⅞ x 7 ¼
3 ¼	1 ⅞	1 ½ + 2 ¾	5 ¼	3 ¼	4 x 7 ⅝
3 ⅜	2	1 ½ + 3	5 ½	3 ¼	4 ⅛ x 7 ⅞
3 ½	2	1 ½ + 3	5 ¾	3 ½	4 ¼ x 9
3 ⅝	2	2 + 3 ¼	6 ¼	4	4 ½ x 9 ⅝
3 ¾	2 ⅛	2 ½ + 3 ¾	6 ½	4	4 ¾ x 10 ⅛
3 ⅞	2 ¼	2 ½ + 4	6 ¾	4 ¼	5 ⅛ x 10 ⅝
4	2 ¼	2 ½ + 4	7	4 ½	5 ¾ x 11

Hints:
- The diamond units can be unusual to work with. The charts are designed to help you with the sizing of the options. Your own personal sewing personality and sewing equipment can alter the sizing of your unit, as well as how well you understand the system and use your ruler. If you need to alter the size, just go up or down the center diamond column.
- This option is cut to create blunt corners when surround strips are added. When looking at the sequence, it is a #18, #4, #1.
- When figuring size from scratch for any design, use the sewn measurements. The large number is where you cut the option apart. It becomes the outside edge in most designs.
- Sewn measurements are the original outside edge of the option.
- Surround strip width can always be cut wider for easy strip cutting.
- When figuring borders, use the sewn measurements.

Option 31

Instructions on page 39.

Cut Size for Center Diamond	Cut Size Surround Strip Row 1	Cut Size Surround Strip Row 2	Unit Cut Size 2nd Round	Cut Size Surround Strip Row 3	Unit Cut Size 3rd Round
1 ⅜	1	1	1 ½	1 ½	2
1 ½	1	1 ⅛	2	1 ½	2 ½
1 ⅝	1 ⅛	1 ⅛	2 ¼	1 ½	2 ⅞
1 ¾	1 ¼	1 ¼	2 ⅝	1 ¾	3 ½
1 ⅞	1 ¼	1 + 1 ¼	2 ¾	1 ¾	3 ¾
2	1 ¼	1 + 1 ¾	3 ⅛	2	4 ¼
2 ⅛	1 ¼	1 + 1 ¾	3 ⅜	2 ¼	4 ½
2 ¼	1 ⅜	1 ¼ + 2	3 ⅝	2 ¼	5
2 ⅜	1 ½	1 ¼ + 2	3 ¾	2 ¼	5 ⅛
2 ½	1 ½	1 ½ + 2 ¼	4 ¼	2 ½	5 ¾
2 ⅝	1 ½	1 ½ + 2 ¼	4 ⅝	2 ¾	6 ¼
2 ¾	1 ⅝	1 ½ + 2 ¼	4 ⅞	2 ¾	6 ½
2 ⅞	1 ¾	1 ½ + 2 ½	5 ⅛	3	6 ¾
3	1 ¾	1 ½ + 3	5 ⅜	3	7 ½
3 ⅛	1 ¾	1 ¾ + 3	5 ¾	3	7 ¾
3 ¼	1 ⅞	1 ¾ + 3	5 ⅞	3 ¼	8 ⅛
3 ⅜	2	2 + 3	6	3 ½	8 ⅜
3 ½	2	2 + 3 ½	6 ¾	3 ¾	9 ½
3 ⅝	2	2 ¼ + 3 ¾	7	4	10 ¼
3 ¾	2 ⅛	2 ¼ + 3 ¾	7 ½	4	10 ½
3 ⅞	2 ¼	2 ¼ + 4	7 ¾	4 ¼	11
4	2 ¼	2 ¼ + 4	8	4 ¼	11 ¼

Hints:
- *The diamond units can be unusual to work with. The charts are designed to help you with the sizing of the options. Your own personal sewing personality and sewing equipment can alter the sizing of your unit, as well as how well you understand the system and use your ruler. If you need to alter the size, just go up or down the center diamond column.*
- *This option is cut to create blunt corners when surround strips are added. When looking at the sequence, it is a #18, #4, #1.*
- *When figuring size from scratch for any design, use the sewn measurements. The large number is where you cut the option apart. It becomes the outside edge in most designs.*
- *Sewn measurements are the original outside edge of the option.*
- *Surround strip width can always be cut wider for easy strip cutting.*
- *When figuring borders, use the sewn measurements.*

Option 30
Father Goose
Instructions on page 38

Cut size of Rectangle Unit	Sewn-finished or graph paper size rectangle	Cut Strip for Center Diamond	Cut Size of Surround Strip Row 1	Cut Size of Surround Strip Row 2	Cut Size of Surround Strip Row 3
1 ½ x 2 ½	1 x 2	1 ⅜	1	1 + 1 ¼	1 ¼
1 ½ x 2 ⅝	1 x 2 ¼	1 ½	1	1 + 1 ¼	1 ¼
1 ⅝ x 3	1 ¼ x 2 ½	1 ⅝	1	1 + 1 ¼	1 ½
2 x 3 ⅝	1 ½ x 3 ⅛	1 ¾	1 ⅛	1 + 1 ½	1 ¾
2 ¼ x 4 ¼	1 ¾ x 3 ¾	1 ⅞	1 ¼	1 ¼ + 1 ½	2
2 ⅜ x 4 ⅜	1 ⅞ x 3 ⅞	2	1 ¼	1 ¼ + 1 ¾	2
2 ⅝ x 4 ¾	2 ⅛ x 4 ¼	2 ⅛	1 ¼	1 ¼ + 1 ¾	2
2 ⅞ x 5 ¼	2 ⅜ x 4 ¾	2 ¼	1 ⅜	1 ¼ + 2	2 ¼
3 x 5 ½	2 ½ x 5	2 ⅜	1 ½	1 ½ + 2	2 ¼
3 ¼ x 6	2 ¾ x 5 ½	2 ½	1 ½	1 ½ + 2 ¼	2 ½
3 ½ x 5 ½	3 x 5	2 ⅝	1 ½	1 ¾ + 2 ½	2 ¾
3 ¾ x 7	3 ¼ x 6 ½	2 ¾	1 ⅝	1 ¾ + 2 ½	3
3 ⅞ x 6 ¼	3 ⅜ x 6 ¾	2 ⅞	1 ¾	1 ¾ + 2 ½	3
4 x 7 ½	3 ½ x 7	3	1 ¾	1 ¾ + 2 ¾	3
4 ½ x 7 ¾	3 ⅝ x 7 ¼	3 ⅛	1 ¾	1 ¾ + 3	3
4 ¼ x 8 ⅜	3 ¾ x 7 ⅞	3 ¼	1 ⅞	2 + 3	3 ¼
4 ½ x 8 ½	4 x 8	3 ⅜	2	2 + 3	3 ½
5 ⅛ x 9 ¾	4 ⅝ x 9 ¼	3 ½	2	2 ¼ + 3 ¼	3 ½
5 ¼ x 10 ¼	4 ¾ x 9 ¾	3 ⅝	2 ⅛	2 ¼ + 3 ¾	3 ¾
5 ½ x 10 ½	5 x 10	3 ¾	2 ⅛	2 ½ + 3 ¾	4
5 ½ x 11	5 x 10 ½	3 ⅞	2 ¼	2 ½ + 4	4 ½
5 ¾ x 11 ⅛	5 ¼ x 10 ⅝	4	2 ¼	2 ½ + 4	4 ½

Hints:
- *The diamond units can be unusual to work with. The charts are designed to help you with the sizing of the options. Your own personal sewing personality and sewing equipment can alter the sizing of your unit, as well as how well you understand the system and use your ruler. If you need to alter the size, just go up or down the center diamond column.*
- *When figuring size from scratch for any design, use the sewn measurements. The large number is where you cut the option apart. It becomes the outside edge in most designs.*
- *Sewn measurements are the original outside edge of the option.*
- *Surround strip width can always be cut wider for easy strip cutting.*
- *When figuring borders, use the sewn measurements.*

Option 29
The Instant Star
Instructions on page 37.

Sewn-Finished or Graph Paper Size Triangle	Cut Strip for Center Diamond	Cut Size of Surround Strip Row 1	Cut Size of Surround Strip Row 2
1 ⅞ x 1 ⅜	1 ⅜	1	¾ + 1 ¼
2 ½ x 1 ¾	1 ½	1	1 ¼ + 1 ½
2 ⅝ x 1 ¾	1 ⅝	1	1 ¼ + 1 ¾
3 x 2 ¼	1 ¾	1 ⅛	1 ¼ + 2
3 ½ x 2 ½	1 ⅞	1 ¼	1 ¼ + 2
3 ½ x 2 ⅝	2	1 ¼	1 ¼ + 2 ¼
4 ½ x 3	2 ⅛	1 ¼	1 ½ + 2 ½
4 ¾ x 3 ⅜	2 ¼	1 ⅜	1 ½ + 2 ½
5 x 3 ½	2 ⅜	1 ½	1 ½ + 2 ½
5 ¾ x 4	2 ½	1 ½	1 ½ + 2 ¾
6 ⅛ x 4 ¼	2 ⅝	1 ½	1 ¾ x 2 ¾
6 ½ x 4 ½	2 ¾	1 ⅝	1 ¾ + 3
6 ⅞ x 4 ¾	2 ⅞	1 ¾	2 + 3
7 x 5	3	1 ¾	2 + 3 ¼
7 ¼ x 5 ¼	3 ⅛	1 ¾	2 + 3 ¼
7 ⅜ x 5 ½	3 ¼	1 ⅞	2 + 3 ¼
8 x 5 ⅜	3 ⅜	2	2 ¼ x 3 ¼
9 x 6 ½	3 ½	2	2 ¼ + 3 ½
9 ¼ x 7	3 ⅝	2 ⅛	2 ¼ + 3 ¾
10 x 7 ¼	3 ¾	2 ⅛	2 ¼ + 3 ¾
10 ⅜ x 7 ½	3 ⅞	2 ¼	2 ½ + 3 ¾
10 ¾ x 8	4	2 ¼	2 ½ + 4

Hints:
- *The diamond units can be unusual to work with. The charts are designed to help you with the sizing of the options. Your own personal sewing personality and sewing equipment can alter the sizing of your unit, as well as how you understand the system and use your ruler. If you need to alter the size, just go up or down the center diamond column.*
- *When figuring size from scratch for any design, use the sewn measurements. The large number is where you cut the option apart. It becomes the outside edge in most designs.*
- *Sewn measurments are the original outside edge of the option.*
- *Surround strip width can always be cut wider for easy strip cutting.*
- *When figuring borders, use the sewn measurements.*
- *Sew a sample to perfect your extenders.*
- *Extender strips are estimated in width. You may go smaller or wider.*

Option 25
Long Legged Ladies
Instructions on page 30.

Cut Size of Rectangle Unit	Sewn-Finished or Graph Paper Size Rectangle	Cut Strip for Center Diamond	Cut Size of Surround Strip Row 1	Top Unit Sewn Size	Side Unit Sewn Size	Top Extender	Side Extender	Block Size
1 ½ x 2 ¼	1 x 1 ¾	1 ⅜	1	⅜	½	2	3	4
1 ¾ x 2 ½	1 ¼ x 2	1 ½	1	½	¾	2	3	5
1 ¾ x 2 ¾	1 ¼ x 2 ¼	1 ⅝	1 ⅛	⅝	⅞	2	3	6
2 x 3	1 ½ x 2 ½	1 ¾	1 ¼	⅞	1	2	3	6
2 x 3 ⅛	1 ½ x 2 ⅝	1 ⅞	1 ¼	1	1 ⅞	2	3	6
2 ¼ x 3 ½	1 ¾ x 3	2	1 ¼	1 ⅛	2	2	3	6
2 ⅜ x 3 ¾	1 ⅞ x 3 ¼	2 ⅛	1 ¼	1 ¼	2	2	3	8
2 ½ x 4	2 x 3 ½	2 ¼	1 ⅜	1 ¾	2 ⅛	2	4	8
2 ⅝ x 4 ¼	2 ⅛ x 3 ¾	2 ⅜	1 ½	1 ⅝	2 ¼	3	4	8
2 ¾ x 4 ½	2 ¼ x 4	2 ½	1 ½	1 ¾	2 ⅞	3	4	9
3 x 4 ¾	2 ½ x 4 ¼	2 ⅝	1 ½	1 ⅞	3	3	4	9
3 ⅛ x 5	2 ⅝ x 4 ¼	2 ¾	1 ⅝	2	3 ⅜	3	4	9
3 ¼ x 5 ⅛	2 ¾ x 4 ⅝	2 ⅞	1 ¾	2 ⅛	3 ⅝	3	4	10
3 ⅜ x 5 ½	2 ⅞ x 5	3	1 ¾	2 ¼	3 ¾	3	4	10
3 ⅜ x 5 ⅝	2 ⅞ x 5 ⅛	3 ⅛	1 ¾	2 ⅜	3 ⅞	3	4	10
3 ½ x 5 ¾	3 x 5 ¼	3 ¼	1 ⅞	2 ½	4 ⅛	3	4	10
3 ¾ x 6 ¼	3 ¼ x 5 ¾	3 ⅜	2	2 ⅝	4 ⅝	3	4	10
4 x 6 ¾	3 ½ x 6 ¼	3 ½	2	2 ⅞	4 ⅞	3	4	11
4 ⅛ x 6 ¾	3 ⅝ x 6 ¼	3 ⅝	2	3	5	3	4	11
4 ¼ x 7 ⅛	3 ¾ x 6 ⅝	3 ¾	2 ⅛	3 ⅛	5 ½	3	4	12
4 ⅜ x 7 ⅛	3 ⅞ x 6 ⅝	3 ⅞	2 ¼	3 ¼	5 ⅝	3	4	12
4 ½ x 7 ½	4 x 7	4	2 ¼	3 ⅜	5 ¾	3	4	12

Hints:
- *Sewn measurements are the original outside edge of the option.*
- *Surround strip width can always be cut wider for easy strip cutting.*
- *When figuring borders use the sewn measurements.*
- *Sew a sample to perfect your extenders.*
- *Extender strips are estimated in width. You may go smaller or wider.*
- *Block size can vary depending on what you want and with the extender width.*

Option 24
Wagon Spokes
Instructions on page 29.

Cut Size of Rectangle Unit	Sewn-Finished or Graph Paper Size Rectangle	Cut Strip for Center Diamond	Cut Size of Surround Strip Row 1	Sewn Size of Cut Angle	Cut Size of Angle	Sewn Long Side	Extender Cut Width	Block Size Up To
1 ½ x 2 ¼	1 x 1 ¾	1 ⅜	1	⅞	1 ¾	1 ¼	2	8
1 ¾ x 2 ½	1 ¼ x 2	1 ½	1	1 ¾	2 ¾	1 ⅜	2	8
1 ¾ x 2 ¾	1 ¼ x 2 ¼	1 ⅝	1 ⅛	1 ⅝	3 ⅛	1 ½	2	8
2 x 3	1 ½ x 2 ½	1 ¾	1 ¼	1 ⅞	3 ½	1 ⅞	2	8
2 x 3 ⅛	1 ½ x 2 ⅝	1 ⅞	1 ¼	2 ⅜	3 ¾	2 ⅛	2	8
2 ¼ x 3 ½	1 ¾ x 3	2	1 ¼	2 ⅞	4	2 ⅜	2	8
2 ⅜ x 3 ¾	1 ⅞ x 3 ¼	2 ⅛	1 ¼	3 ¼	4 ¼	2 ⅝	2	8
2 ½ x 4	2 x 3 ½	2 ¼	1 ⅜	3 ⅜	4 ½	2 ⅞	2 ½	10
2 ⅝ x 4 ¼	2 ⅛ x 3 ¾	2 ⅜	1 ½	3 ⅝	4 ⅞	3	2 ½	12
2 ¾ x 4 ½	2 ¼ x 4	2 ½	1 ½	3 ⅞	5 ⅜	3 ⅜	2 ½	14
3 x 4 ¾	2 ½ x 4 ¼	2 ⅝	1 ½	4 ⅜	5 ⅝	3 ¾	3	14
3 ⅛ x 5	2 ⅝ x 4 ¼	2 ¾	1 ⅝	4 ⅝	6	4	3	14
3 ¼ x 5 ⅛	2 ¾ x 4 ⅝	2 ⅞	1 ¾	4 ¾	6 ⅛	4 ⅛	3	14
3 ⅜ x 5 ½	2 ⅞ x 5	3	1 ¾	5 ⅛	6 ⅜	4 ⅜	3	14
3 ⅜ x 5 ⅝	2 ⅞ x 5 ⅛	3 ⅛	1 ¾	5 ¼	6 ½	4 ½	3 ½	15
3 ½ x 5 ¾	3 x 5 ¼	3 ¼	1 ⅞	5 ⅝	7	4 ¾	3 ½	16
3 ¾ x 6 ¼	3 ¼ x 5 ¾	3 ⅜	2	6	7 ¼	5	4	18
4 x 6 ¾	3 ½ x 6 ¼	3 ½	2	6 ⅛	7 ⅜	5 ¼	4	18
4 ⅛ x 6 ¾	3 ⅝ x 6 ¼	3 ⅝	2	6 ⅜	7 ¾	5 ½	4 ½	20
4 ¼ x 7 ⅛	3 ¾ x 6 ⅝	3 ¾	2 ⅛	6 ⅞	8	5 ¾	5	22
4 ⅜ x 7 ⅛	3 ⅞ x 6 ⅝	3 ⅞	2 ¼	7 ⅛	8 ⅜	6	5	22
4 ½ x 7 ½	4 x 7	4	2 ¼	7 ¼	8 ½	6 ⅛	5	23

Hints:
- Surround strip width can always be cut wider for easy strip cutting.
- Row 2 surround strips have two width sizes. The smaller one is for the top and bottom of the rectangle / diamond unit.
- This chart gives you cut measurements of the unit each time you sew around with a row of strips. When looking for the size you need, you may need to back it down to the sewn size.
- The sewn long side is column 7 (Fig A).
- Sewn size of the cut angle is column 5 (Fig B).
- Block size can vary depending on what you want and with the extender width.
- Sew a sample to perfect your extenders.
- Extender strips are estimated in width. You may go smaller or wider.

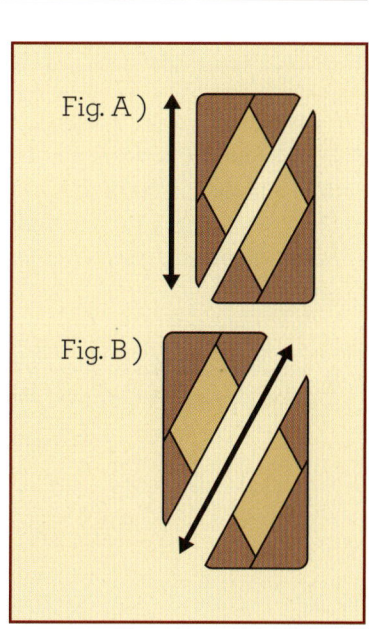

Fig. A)

Fig. B)

Option 22
The Diamond Twist
Instructions on page 27.

Cut Size of Rectangle Unit	Sewn-Finished or Graph Paper Size Rectangle	Cut Strip for Center Diamond	Cut Size of Surround Strip Row 1	Cut Size of Surround Strip Row 2	Unit Cut Size 2nd Round	Cut Size of Surround Strip Row 3	Unit Cut Size 3rd Round	Cut Size Surround Strip Row 4	Unit Cut Size 4th Round
1 ½ x 2 ¼	1 x 1 ¾	1 ⅜	1	1 ¼	2 ¼ x 2 ⅝	1 ½	3 ⅛ x 3 ¼	2	4 ⅜
1 ¾ x 2 ½	1 ¼ x 2	1 ½	1	1 ¼	2 ⅝	1 ½	3 ½ x 3 ½	2	4 ⅝
1 ¾ x 2 ¾	1 ¼ x 2 ¼	1 ⅝	1 ⅛	1 ¼ + 1 ½	2 ⅝ x 3	1 ½	3 ⅝ x 4	2	4 ⅞
2 x 3	1 ½ x 2 ½	1 ¾	1 ¼	1 ¼ + 1 ¾	3 x 3 ⅛	1 ¾	3 ⅝ x 4	2	5 ½ x 5 ¾
2 x 3 ⅛	1 ½ x 2 ⅝	1 ⅞	1 ¼	1 ¼ + 1 ¾	3 ¼ x 3 ⅝	1 ¾	4 ½ x 4 ⅝	2 ¼	6 x 6 ½
2 ¼ x 3 ½	1 ¾ x 3	2	1 ¼	1 ¼ + 1 ¾	3 ⅞ x 4	2 ¼	5 x 5 ⅛	2 ½	6 ⅜ x 6 ⅝
2 ⅜ x 3 ¾	1 ⅞ x 3 ¼	2 ⅛	1 ¼	1 ¼ + 1 ¾	3 ⅞ x 4 ¼	2 ¼	5 ⅛ x 5 ¼	2 ¾	6 ¾ x 7
2 ½ x 4	2 x 3 ½	2 ¼	1 ⅜	1 ¼ + 2	4 x 4 ⅜	2 ¼	5 ½ x 5 ⅝	2 ¾	7 ⅜
2 ⅝ x 4 ¼	2 ⅛ x 3 ¾	2 ⅜	1 ½	1 ¼ + 2	4 ⅛ x 4 ⅝	2 ¼	5 ⅝ x 6	3	7 ¾
2 ¾ x 4 ½	2 ¼ x 4	2 ½	1 ½	1 ¾ + 2 ¼	4 ½ x 5	2 ½	6 ½ x 6 ½	3 ¼	8 ¾
3 x 4 ¾	2 ½ x 4 ¼	2 ⅝	1 ½	1 ¾ + 2 ¼	4 ⅞ x 5 ½	2 ¾	6 ⅞ x 7 ⅛	3 ¼	9 ¼
3 ⅛ x 5	2 ⅝ x 4 ¼	2 ¾	1 ⅝	1 ¾ + 2 ¼	5 ⅛ x 5 ⅝	2 ¾	7 x 7 ¼	3 ¼	9 ½
3 ¼ x 5 ⅛	2 ¾ x 4 ⅝	2 ⅞	1 ¾	1 ¾ + 2 ½	5 ¼ x 6	3	7 ½ x 7 ¾	3 ½	10 x 10 ⅛
3 ⅜ x 5 ½	2 ⅞ x 5	3	1 ¾	1 ¾ + 2 ½	5 ½ x 6	3	7 ¾ x 7 ¾	4	10 ¼
3 ⅜ x 5 ⅝	2 ⅞ x 5 ⅛	3 ⅛	1 ¾	1 ¾ + 2 ½	5 ½ x 6 ¾	3	7 ¾ x 8	4	10 ¼ x 10 ½
3 ½ x 5 ¾	3 x 5 ¼	3 ¼	1 ⅞	1 ¾ + 3	6 x 6 ¾	3	8 ⅜ x 8 ⅝	4	11 ¼ x 12
3 ¾ x 6 ¼	3 ¼ x 5 ¾	3 ⅜	2	2 + 3	6 ¼ x 7	3 ¼	8 ¾ x 9	4 ¼	12 x 12 ⅝
4 x 6 ¾	3 ½ x 6 ¼	3 ½	2	2 + 3 ¼	6 ⅜ x 7 ¼	3 ½	8 ⅞ x 9	4 ½	12 ¼
4 ⅛ x 6 ¾	3 ⅝ x 6 ¼	3 ⅝	2	2 ⅛ + 3 ¼	6 ¾ x 7 ⅝	3 ½	9 ½ x 9 ¾	4 ½	12 ¾ x 13
4 ¼ x 7 ⅛	3 ¾ x 6 ⅝	3 ¾	2 ⅛	2 ¼ + 3 ¼	7 x 8	3 ½	10 x 10 ¼	5 ½	13 ½
4 ⅜ x 7 ⅛	3 ⅞ x 6 ⅝	3 ⅞	2 ¼	2 ¼ + 3 ½	7 ¼ x 8 ¼	3 ¾	10 ⅛ x 10 ½	5 ¾	13 ¾ x 14
4 ½ x 7 ½	4 x 7	4	2 ¼	2 ¼ + 3 ½	7 ½ x 8 ½	4	10 ⅝ x 11	6	14 ½

Hints:
- *When using the diamond twist it may not always be a perfect square. Use the column on the chart that states unit cut size. Also note how many times you sew around the center.*
- *Surround strip width can always be cut wider for easy strip cutting.*
- *Row 2 surround strips have two width sizes. The smaller one is for the top and bottom of rectangle/diamond unit.*
- *When figuring sizes from scratch, remember that the sewn measurement is what you must work with.*
- *This chart gives you cut measurements of the unit each time you sew around with a row of strips. When looking for the size you need, you may need to back it down to the sewn size.*

Option 21 (cont.)

Unit Cut Size with 2nd Round	Cut Size Surround Strip Row 3	Unit Cut Size with 3rd Round	Cut Size Surround Strip Row 4	Unit Cut Size with 4th Row
2 ½	1 ½	3 ½	2	4 ⅝
2 ⅝	1 ½	3 ¾	2 ⅛	5
3	1 ¾	4	2 ¼	5 ½
3 ¼	2	4 ½	2 ¾	6
3 ½	2	4 ¾	2 ¾	6 ½
3 ¾	2	5 ⅛	3	7
4 ⅛	2 ¼	5 ¾	3 ¼	7 ¾
4 ⅜	2 ⅜	6	3 ½	8 ⅛
4 ½	2 ½	6	3 ⅝	8 ⅜
5	2 ½	6 ¾	3 ¾	9 ⅜
5 ¼	2 ⅞	7 ¼	4	10
5 ½	3	7 ⅝	4 ¼	10 ⅝
5 ¾	3	7 ⅞	4 ¼	10 ⅞
6	3 ⅛	8	4 ¼	11 ¼
6 ⅛	3 ¼	8 ⅜	4 ½	11 ½
6 ½	3 ⅜	9	4 ¾	12 ¼
6 ¾	3 ¾	9 ⅝	5	13 ¼
7 ⅛	4	9 ¾	5 ¼	13 ½
7 ½	4 ¼	10 ½	5 ½	14 ½
7 ¾	4 ¼	10 ¾	5 ½	15
8 ⅛	4 ¼	11 ⅛	6	15 ½
8 ¼	4 ⅜	11 ⅜	6	16

Option 21

Instructions on page 26.

Cut size of Rectangle Unit	Sewn-finished or graph paper size rectangle	Cut Strip for Center Diamond	Cut Size of Surround Strip Row 1	Cut Size of Surround Strip Row 2
1 ½ x 2 ¼	1 x 1 ¾	1 ⅜	1	1 + 1 ½
1 ¾ x 2 ½	1 ¼ x 2	1 ½	1	1 + 1 ¾
1 ¾ x 2 ¾	1 ¼ x 2 ¼	1 ⅝	1 ⅛	1 + 1 ¾
2 x 3	1 ½ x 2 ½	1 ¾	1 ¼	1 + 1 ¾
2 x 3 ⅛	1 ½ x 2 ⅝	1 ⅞	1 ¼	1 ¼ + 1 ¾
2 ¼ x 3 ½	1 ¾ x 3	2	1 ¼	1 ¼ + 2
2 ⅜ x 3 ¾	1 ⅞ x 3 ¼	2 ⅛	1 ¼	1 ¼ + 2
2 ½ x 4	2 x 3 ½	2 ¼	1 ⅜	1 ½ + 2
2 ⅝ x 4 ¼	2 ⅛ x 3 ¾	2 ⅜	1 ½	1 ½ + 2 ¼
2 ¾ x 4 ½	2 ¼ x 4	2 ½	1 ½	1 ½ + 2 ½
3 x 4 ¾	2 ½ x 4 ¼	2 ⅝	1 ½	1 ¾ + 2 ½
3 ⅛ x 5	2 ⅝ x 4 ¼	2 ¾	1 ⅝	1 ¾ + 2 ⅝
3 ¼ x 5 ⅛	2 ¾ x 4 ⅝	2 ⅞	1 ¾	1 ¾ + 2 ¾
3 ⅜ x 5 ½	2 ⅞ x 5	3	1 ¾	1 ⅞ + 2 ¾
3 ⅜ x 5 ⅝	2 ⅞ x 5 ⅛	3 ⅛	1 ¾	2 + 3
3 ½ x 5 ¾	3 x 5 ¼	3 ¼	1 ⅞	2 + 3
3 ¾ x 6 ¼	3 ¼ x 5 ¾	3 ⅜	2	2 + 3 ¼
4 x 6 ¾	3 ½ x 6 ¼	3 ½	2	2 ¼ + 3 ½
4 ⅛ x 6 ¾	3 ⅝ x 6 ¼	3 ⅝	2	2 ½ + 3 ¾
4 ¼ x 7 ⅛	3 ¾ x 6 ⅝	3 ¾	2 ⅛	2 ½ + 4
4 ⅜ x 7 ⅛	3 ⅞ x 6 ⅝	3 ⅞	2 ¼	2 ½ + 4
4 ½ x 7 ½	4 x 7	4	2 ¼	2 ¾ + 4 ¼

Hints:
- When using this option it may not always be a perfect square.
- Surround strip width can always be cut wider for easy strip cutting.
- Row 2 surround strips have two width sizes. The smaller one is for the top and bottom of rectangle/diamond unit.
- When figuring sizes from scratch, remember that the sewn measurement is what you must work with.
- This chart gives you cut measurements of the unit each time you sew around with a row of strips. When looking for the size you need, you may need to back it down to the sewn size.

Option 19
Long Thin Triangle
Instructions on page 24.

Cut Size of Individual Long Thin Triangle	Sewn Size of Individual Long Thin Triangle	Cut Size of Individual Center Diamond Strip	Cut Size for Surround Strip of Center Diamond
1F x ⅞	½F x ⅜	1 ¾	1 ⅛
1 ¼F x 1	¾F x ½	2	1 ¼
1 ½F x 1 ⅛	1F x ⅝	2 ¼	1 ⅜
1 ¾S x 1 ¼	1 ¼S x ¾	2 ½	1 ½
2 x 1 ⅜	1 ½ x ⅞	2 ¾	1 ⅝
2 ⅛ x 1 ½	1 ⅝ x 1	2 ⅞	1 ¾
2 ⅜S x 1 ⅝	1 ⅞F x 1 ⅛	3 ¼	1 ⅞
2 ⅝F x 1 ¾	2 ⅛F x 1 ¼	3 ⅜	2
2 ⅞F x 1 ⅞	2 ⅜F x 1 ⅜	3 ½	2
3 ⅛ x 2	2 ⅝ x 1 ½	3 ¾	2 ⅛
3 ¼F x 2 ⅛	2 ¾ x 1 ⅝	4	2 ¼
3 ½F x 2 ¼	3 x 1 ¾	4 ¼	2 ⅜

Option 20
Roof Top Triangles
Instructions on page 25.

Cut Size of Individual Roof Top Retangle	Sewn Size of Individual Roof Top Rectangle	Cut Size of Center Diamond Strip	Cut Size of Surround Strip of Center Diamond
1 ¼ x ¾	¾ x ¼	1 ⅜	1
1 ⅝ x ⅞	1 ⅛ x ⅜	1 ½	1
2 x 1	1 ½ x ½	1 ¾	1 ⅛
2 ½ x 1F	2 x ½F	2	1 ¼
3 x 1 ¼	2 ½ x ¾	2 ¼	1 ⅜
3 ½ x 1 ⅜	3 x ⅞	2 ½	1 ½
4 x 1 ½F	3 ½ x 1	2 ¾	1 ⅝
4 ½F x 1 ⅝	3 ¾ x 1 ⅛	2 ⅞	1 ¾
5 x 1 ⅞	4 ½ x 1 ⅜	3 ¼*	1 ⅞
5 ¼ x 2S	4 ¾ x 1 ½	3 ⅜*	2
5 ½ x 2	5 x 1 ½	3 ½*	2
6 x 2 ⅛	5 ½ x 1 ⅞	3 ¾	2 ⅛

Squares per Strip
(based on a 40" strip, cut selvedge to selvedge)

Strip Width	Number of Squares
1"	40
1 ¼"	32
1 ½"	26
1 ¾"	22
2"	20
2 ¼"	17
2 ½"	16
2 ¾"	14
3"	13
3 ¼"	12
3 ½"	11
3 ¾"	10
4"	10
4 ¼"	9
4 ½"	8
4 ¾"	8
5"	8

Fractions into Decimals

⅛	.125
¼	.25
⅜	.375
½	.5
⅝	.625
¾	.75
⅞	.875

QUICK TIP
In these charts:
F = full, which is slightly larger, either cut or sewn
S = scant, which is slightly smaller, either cut or sewn.

QUICK TIP
Depending on your personal private measurements (PPM) you may need to slightly trim your Option 4 pinwheel units. Sew a test pinwheel.

Option 18
Canadian Geese
Instructions on page 23.

Sewn (finished) Size	Cut (unfinished) Size	Cut Strip for Center Diamond	Cut Strip Size
¾ x ⅝	1 ¼ x 1 ⅛	1 ⅜	1
1 x ¾	1 ½ x 1 ¼	1 ½	1
1 ¼ x 1	1 ¾ x 1 ½	1 ¾	1 ⅛
1 ½ x 1 ¼	2 x 1 ¾	2	1 ¼
1 ¾ x 1 ½	2 ¼ x 2	2 ¼	1 ⅜
2 x 1 ¾	2 ½ x 2 ¼	2 ½	1 ½
2 ¼ x 2	2 ¾ x 2 ½	2 ¾	1 ⅝
2 ½ x 2 ¼	3 x 2 ⅝	2 ⅞	1 ¾
2 ¾ x 2 ⅜	3 ¼ x 2 ⅞	3 ¼	1 ⅞
3 x 2 ⅝	3 ½ x 3 ⅛	3 ⅜	2
3 ¼ x 2 ⅞	3 ¾ x 3 ⅜	3 ½	2
3 ½ x 3	4 x 3 ½	3 ¾	2 ⅛
3 ¾ x 3 ¼	4 ¼ x 3 ¾	4	2 ¼
4 x 3 ½	4 ½ x 4	4 ¼	2 ⅜

QUICK TIP *basic square:*
- use short strips on the sides when possible
- no more than a finger space is needed between squares when strip piecing
- strive for 25 to 50 basic squares per hour to optimize the speed of the system
- the small fabric pieces that are trimmed off the basic square can be used in many ways but the larger pieces can be recycled and used as surround strips; use your imagination for your scraps

QUICK TIP *troubleshooting:*
If your option is too large or small, double check:
- the center square size
- seam allowance
- the way you lay your ruler on the sewn square

QUICK TIP
Notice how some of the diamond strip sizes are only ⅛" apart in size. This makes the long side of the roof top change, but not the short side. If you need a size not on the chart, find the closest one on the chart and adjust the diamond strip size up or down to create the desired size.

Definitions
The following list of commonly used terms will help you better understand how to use charts and instructions throughout this book.

OPTIONS
Cut square, triangle or rectangle units of the Square in a Square® system. It is not an Option until the basic squares and strips have been sewn and trimmed accordingly.

UNITS
Several geometric shapes and/or Options sewn together.

BLOCKS
Several units sewn together. Multiple blocks sewn together make up most quilt tops.

SCANT
A seam allowance a few threads less than a full ¼" allowing you to press the fabric open without changing the size of the unit or block.

CUT
Pertains to the size of a pattern piece with the seam allowance included. Also referred to as "raw" or "unfinished" size.

SEWN
Pertains to a unit or block once completed. Also referred to as "finished" or "graph paper" size.

PIGS
An acronym that stands for Projects In Grocery Sacks. These are sewing projects not yet completed and placed in bags or boxes for safe keeping. A Pig Pen is the location such as a shelf, under a bed or in a closet where multiple PIGS are stored. Some PIGS have even been known to be corraled in campers and freezers. When multiple Pig Pens are established in one location, this is called a Stockyard. Left unattended, the Stockyard will begin to stink and squeal, causing stifled creativity and the inability to purchase or begin new projects. Also referred to as UFOs (Unfinished Projects). Use and knowledge of the Square in a Square® system will help eliminate PIGS and keep them from returning or inviting unwanted friends.

Crossroads

Crossroads

Difficulty: Beginner

Quilt Size: 27"x 32"

Square in a Square® Technique: Option 21

This is an easy quilt for beginners to learn the diamond option technique. It is a great quilt to help diminish your stash and finish quickly. You can create additional looks by changing color placement. So, have fun mixing things up!

Fabric

The following amounts are for the entire quilt.

Background: ⅔ yd
Yellow: ⅔ yd
Brown: ⅓ yd
Red: ¼ yd
Scrappy Light Print: ¼ yd
Inner Border: Brown Print ¼ yd
Outer Border: Yellow Print ⅓ yd

Cut

The following measurements are for cutting the entire quilt. The number in parentheses is the number of pieces that need to be cut. Strips are to be cut the full width of your fabric or selvedge to selvedge. Be sure to label and keep all of your pieces together. The numbers in the circles ❶ after each cutting, correspond with the sewing steps.

Background: ⅔ yd
(2) 2 ½" strips cut into (20) 2 ½" center diamonds ❶
(3) 2 ½" surround strips for Block B, row 2, long sides ❷

Yellow: ⅔ yd
(7) 1 ½" surround strips for row 1 ❶
(4) 2 ½" strips for outer border ❹

Brown: ⅓ yd
(2) 1 ½" surround strips for Block B, row 2, short sides ❷
(4) 1 ½" strips for inner border ❹

Red: ¼ yd
(2) 1 ½" surround strips for Block A, row 2, short sides ❷
(4) 2 ½" squares for border ❹
(4) 2 ½" corner squares (cut first across the end of fabric) ❸

Scrappy Light Print: ¼ yd
(3) 2 ½" surround strips for Block A, row 2, long sides ❷

Inner Border: Brown Print ¼ yd
(4) 1 ½" strips ❸

Blaze

Fabric

The following amounts are for the entire quilt.

Red: 1 yd
Green: 1 ¾ yds
Yellow: 1 ½ yds
Red Floral: 1 ½ yds
Backing: 3 yds
Binding: ½ yd

Cut

The following measurements are for cutting the entire quilt. The number in parentheses is the number of pieces that need to be cut. Strips are to be cut the full width of your fabric or selvedge to selvedge. Be sure to label and keep all of your pieces together. The numbers in the circles ❶ after each cutting, correspond with the sewing steps.

Red: 1 yd
(7) 1 ⅜" strips for 4-Patch ❶
(3) 2" strips into (54) 2" center squares for Option 1 ❷
(6) 2" strips for inner border ❺

Green: 1 ¾ yds
(7) 1 ⅜" strips for 4-Patch ❶
(26) 1 ½" surround strips for Option 7 ❸

Yellow: 1 ½ yds
(14) 1 ⅜" strips for 4-Patch ❶
(14) 1 ¼" surround strips for Option 1 ❷
(6) 1 ½" strips for middle border ❺

Red Floral: 1 ½ yds
(8) 2 ¼" strips into (93) 2 ¼" center diamonds for Option 7 ❸
(6) 4 ½" strips for outer border ❺

Blaze

Difficulty: Intermediate

Quilt Size: 42"x 62"

Square in a Square® Technique: Options 1, 7 and 4-Patch

The Option 7 diamond unit from this system allows you to have intricate quilt designs without the hassle of diamonds, y-seams or set-in pieces. Just a blaze of simplicity with speed and accuracy.

Sew

1. Sew 1 ⅜" strips from yellow and 1 ⅜" strips from green together. Use the 4-Patch Ruler to crosscut the strata into 1 ⅜" units. Repeat for a total of (160) units. Sew into (80) 4-Patch units.
   Sew 1 ⅜"" strips from red and 1 ⅜" strips from yellow together. Use the 4-Patch Ruler to crosscut the strata into 1 ⅜" units. Repeat for a total of (160) units. Sew into (80) 4-Patch units.
   Sew the 4-Patch units into (40) double 4-Patch blocks.
   Watch how the colors run diagonally through the block.
2. Sew and cut (54) Option 1s using 2" center squares from red and 1 ¼" surround strips from yellow.
3. Sew and cut (93) Option 7s using 2 ¼" center diamonds from red floral and 1 ½" surround strips from green.
4. Sew (9) rows together alternating Option 1 units from step 2 and Option 7 horizontal units from step 3.
   Sew (8) rows together alternating Option 7 vertical unit from step 3 and double 4-Patch from step 1. Sew rows together.
5. Sew the 2" strips from red for inner border into long strips. Sew the long sides of the border to the quilt first, then add the top and bottom.
   Sew the 1 ½" strips from yellow for middle border into long strips. Sew the long sides of the border to the quilt first, then add the top and bottom.
   Sew the 4 ½" strips from red floral for outer border into long strips. Sew the long sides of the border to the quilt first, then add the top and bottom.

Cathedral Star

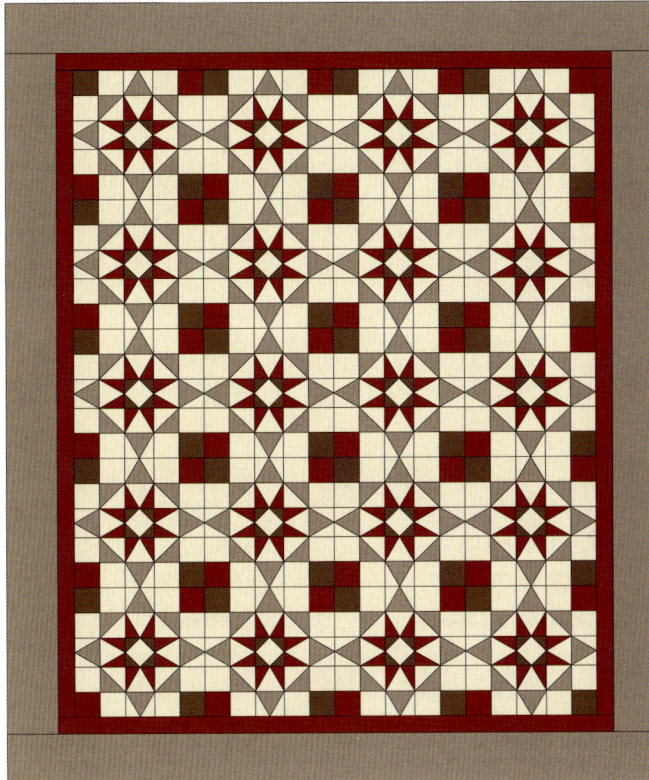

Cathedral Star

Difficulty: Intermediate

Quilt Size: 46"x 55"

Block Size: 7 ¾" cut, 7 ¼" sewn

Block Quantity: 20

Square in a Square® Technique: Options 1, 4 and Option 18

Old churches are so unique and inspiring; the architecture, the bell towers, the eaves, and the stained glass all call out to be made into a quilt block. This block reminds me of one of those beautiful cathedrals. The movement of the diamonds really add depth to this quilt.

Three additional block sizes are given at the end of this pattern.

Fabric

The following amounts are for the entire quilt.

Background: 2 ½ yds
Small Brown Print: ¾ yd
Red: 1 ½ yds
Large Brown Print: 2 yds
Backing: 3 yds
Binding: ½ yd

Cut

The following measurements are for cutting the entire quilt. The number in parentheses is the number of pieces that need to be cut. Strips are to be cut the full width of your fabric or selvedge to selvedge. Be sure to label and keep all of your pieces together. The numbers in the circles ❶ after each cutting, correspond with the sewing steps.

Background: 2 ½ yds
(2) 2" strips into (20) 2" center squares for Option 1 ❶
(3) 3 ⅝" strips into (20) 3 ⅝" center squares for Option 4 ❷
(4) 2 ½" strips into (40) 2 ½" center diamonds for Option 18 ❸
(16) 1 ½" surround strips for Option 18 ❹
(10) 2 ¼" strips into (160) 2 ¼" corner squares ❺

Small Brown Print: 1 ¼ yd
(6) 1 ¼" surround strips for Option 1 ❶
(3) 2 ¼" strips into (40) 2 ¼" corner squares ❺

Red: 1 ½ yds
(16) 1 ½" surround strips for Option 18 ❸
(3) 2 ¼" strips into (40) 2 ¼" corner squares ❺
(5) 1 ½" strips for inner border ⓫

Large Brown Print: 2 yds
(10) 2 ¼" surround strips for Option 4 ❷
(4) 2 ½" strips into (40) center diamonds for Option 18 ❹
(5) 4 ½" strips for outer border ⓫

Sew

❶ Sew and cut (20) Option 1s using 2" center squares from background and 1 ¼" surround strips from small brown print.

❷ Sew and cut (20) Option 4 half-square triangles using a 3 ⅝" center square from background and 2 ¼" surround strips from large brown floral.

❸ Sew and cut (40) Option 18s using 2 ½" center diamonds from background and 1 ½" surround strips from red.
Yields (80) Option 18, Canadian Geese units.

❹ Sew and cut (40) Option 18s using 2 ½" center diamonds from large brown print and 1 ½" surround strips from background.
Yields (80) Option 18, Canadian Geese units.

❺ Sew (1) 2 ¼" red corner square and (2) 2 ¼" background squares together with (1) half-square triangle unit from step 2. Repeat for a total of (40) units.
Sew (1) 2 ¼" small brown print corner square and (2) 2 ¼" background squares together with (1) half-square triangle unit from step 2. Repeat for a total of (40) units.

❻ Sew (1) Canadian Goose from step 3 to (1) Canadian Goose from step 4 together. Repeat for a total of (80) units

❼ Sew (2) units from step 5 and (1) unit from step 6 together. Repeat for a total of (40) sections.

❽ Sew (2) units from step 6 and (1) Option 1 from step 1 together. Repeat for a total of (20) sections.

❾ Sew (2) sections from step 7 and (1) section from step 8 together. Repeat for a total of (20) quilt blocks.

❿ Sew (4) star blocks from step 9 together in a row.
Repeat for (5) rows. Sew all rows together.

⓫ Sew inner border using 1 ½" red strips. Sew the long sides of the border to the quilt first, then add the top and bottom. Sew outer border using 4 ½" large brown floral strips. Sew the long sides of the border to the quilt first, then add the top and bottom.

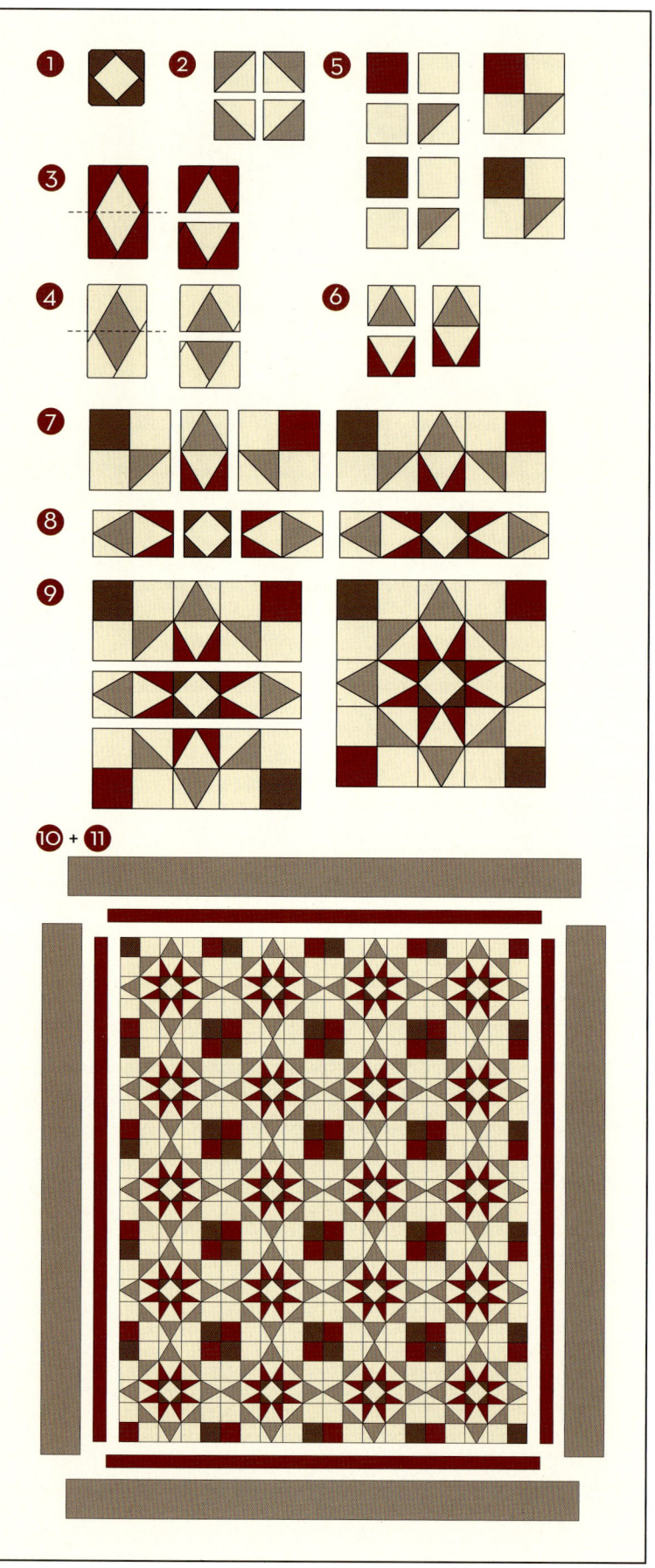

Cathedral Star Variations

Fabric 1: ▣ Fabric 2: ▣ Fabric 3: ▢

The Cathedral Star Block can be sewn in many block sizes. It is one of the main star blocks with an additional row on all four sides of the star.

Sew the star together. Next, sew three sections together for each side and attach to the star. Last, sew top and bottom row together and then sew to main star block.

The sizes below show cut amounts to complete popular sizes of the Cathedral Star block. Please refer to the previous main star charts to adapt your Cathedral Star to whatever size or look you prefer.

The fabric amounts listed below will yield approximately (12) Cathedral Star Blocks.

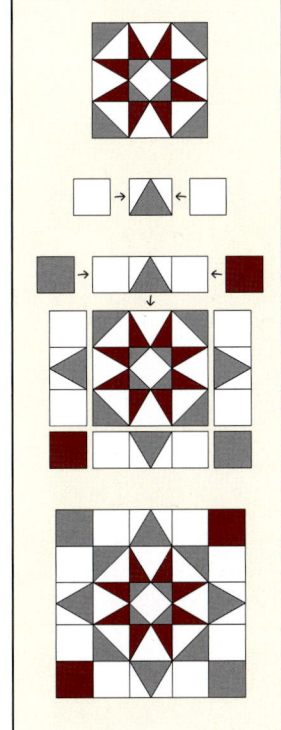

Block Size:	4 ½" cut, 4" sewn
Main Star – sewn 2 ½" cut 3" Cathedral Star – sewn 4" cut 4 ½"	
Fabric 1	1 ¼" solid corner squares
	¾" surround strips for Opt. #1
	2 ½" center squares for Opt. #4
	1 ½" center diamonds for Opt. #18
Fabric 2	1 ¼" solid corner squares
	1" surround strips for Opt. #18
Fabric 3	1 ¼" center squares for Opt. #1
	1 ½" surround strips for Opt. #4
	1 ¼" solid squares
	1" surround strips for Opt. #18
	1 ½" center diamond for Opt. #18
Fabric	⅛ yd diamond
	⅛ yd diamond points
	¼ yd for 12 solid squares

Block Size:	9 ½" cut, 9" sewn
Main Star – sewn 5 ½" cut 6" Cathedral Star – sewn 9" cut 9 ½"	
Fabric 1	2 ¼" solid corner squares
	1 ¼" surround strips for Opt. #1
	3 ⅝" center squares for Opt. #4
	2 ½" center diamonds for Opt. #18
Fabric 2	2 ¼" solid corner squares
	1 ½" surround strips for Opt. #18
Fabric 3	2" center squares for Opt. #1
	2 ⅛" surround strips for Opt. #4
	2 ¼" solid squares
	1 ½" surround strips for Opt. #18
	2 ½" center diamond for Opt. #18
Fabric	⅔ yd diamond Fabric 1
	½ yd diamond points Fabric 2
	1 ¼ yd for 12 solid squares Fabric 3

Block Size: 18 ½" cut, 18" sewn		
Main Star – sewn 11 cut 11 ½" Cathedral Star – sewn 18" cut 18 ½"		
Fabric 1		4" solid corner squares
		1 ⅞" surround strips for Opt. #1
		6 ⅛" center squares for Opt. #4
		4 ¼" center diamonds for Opt. #18
Fabric 2		4" solid corner squares
		2 ⅜" surround strips for Opt. #18
Fabric 3		3 ⅜" center squares for Opt. #1
		3 ½" surround strips for Opt. #4
		4" solid squares
		2 ⅜" surround strips for Opt. #18
		4 ¼" center diamond for Opt. #18

Fabric	
	1 ½ yd diamond Fabric 1
	½ yd diamond points Fabric 2
	1 ½ yd for 12 solid squares Fabric 3

Poinsettia Star

Poinsettia Star

Difficulty: Intermediate

Quilt Size: 70"x 70"

Block Size: 11 ¾" cut, 11 ¼" sewn

Block Quantity: 13

Square in a Square® Technique: Options 3, 4, 11 and Option 18

What a beautiful quilt block! Adding the extra units to the corners of this star really gives it exceptional pizzazz. It may look complicated but once again the Square in a Square system makes it a snap.

Hint: Watch your color placement carefully on your sewing steps as well as your option trimming on steps 2, 4 and 5.

Three additional block sizes are given at the end of this pattern.

Fabric

The following amounts are for the entire quilt.

Background: 3 ½ yds
Red: 2 ¼ yds
Green: 1 ¾ yds
Green Floral: 1 ½ yds border
Backing: 4 ½ yds
Binding: ¾ yd

Cut

The following measurements are for cutting the entire quilt. The number in parentheses is the number of pieces that need to be cut. Strips are to be cut the full width of your fabric or selvedge to selvedge. Be sure to label and keep all of your pieces together. The numbers in the circles ① after each cutting, correspond with the sewing steps.

Background: 3 ½ yds
(3) 3 ⅜" strips into (26) 3 ⅜" center diamonds for Option 18 ②
(9) 3 ¼" surround strips for Option 11, row 2 ③
(4) 2 ¾" strips into (52) 2 ¾" center squares for Option 3 ④
(3) 1 ⅞" strips into (52) 1 ⅞" corner squares ⑤
(3) 3 ½" strips into (52) 1 ⅞" x 3 ½" rectangles ⑥
(4) 11 ¾" strips into (12) 11 ¾" setting squares ⑩

Red: 2 ¼ yds
(2) 3 ⅜" strips into (13) 3 ⅜" center squares for Option 4 ①
(7) 2" surround strips for Option 18 ②
(6) 2 ¼" surround strips for Option 11, row 1 ③
(10) 1 ¾" surround strips for Option 3 ④
(6) 2 ½" strips for inner border ⑩

Green: 1 ¾ yds
(6) 2" surround strips for Option 4 ①
(7) 2" surround strips for Option 18 ②
(2) 3 ⅝" strips into (13) 3 ⅝" center squares for Option 11 ③
(10) 1 ¾" surround strips for Option 3 ④

Green Floral: 1 ½ yds border
(8) 5 ½" strips for outer border ⑩

Sew

① Sew and cut (13) Option 4 half-square triangles using a 3 ⅜" center square from red and 2" surround strips from green.
Sew the units into (13) pinwheel blocks.
Watch color placement carefully. Color location will need to match step 2, Option 18 units.

100

❷ Sew and cut (26) Option 18s using 3 ⅜" center diamonds from background and 2" surround strips from red and green. Sew the same color on opposite sides of the diamond.
Hint: watch color placement carefully. Color location will need to match step 1, pinwheel blocks.

❸ Sew and cut (13) Option 11s using 3 ⅝" center squares from green and 2 ¼" surround strips from red for row one. Use 3 ¼" surround strips from background for row two.

❹ Sew and cut (52) Option 3s using a 2 ¾" center square from background and 1 ¾" surround strips from red and 1 ¾" surround strips from green. Repeat for a total of (104) Option 3 flying geese. Watch color placement carefully. The same fabric should be opposite from each other. When trimming, divide the flying geese into two groups. Trim one group with the green print on the right and the second group with the red print on the right. Repeat for a total of (52) in each trim group.

❺ Sew (1) 1 ⅞" corner square from background to Option 3, flying goose unit from step 4. Repeat for a total of (52) units. Sew (1) Option 11 from step 3 to (1) Option 3 from step 4 together. Sew unit together. Repeat for a total of (52) units. Watch color placement carefully.

❻ Sew a 1 ⅞" x 3 ½" rectangle from background to each Option 18 from step 2. Repeat for a total of (52).

❼ Sew (2) units from step 6 to (1) pinwheel unit from step 1. Repeat for a total of (13) units. Watch color placement carefully.

❽ Sew (1) section from step 6 to (2) units from step 5 together. Repeat for a total of (26) sections.

❾ Sew (1) section from step 7 to (2) sections from step 8. Repeat for a total of (13) blocks.

❿ Sew blocks to 11 ¾" background setting squares, 5 across and 5 down.
Sew the 2 ½" strips from red for the inner border into long strips. Sew the long sides of the border to the quilt first, then add the top and bottom. Repeat for the 5 ½" strips from green floral for the outer border.

Poinsettia Star Variations

Fabric 1:   Fabric 2:   Fabric 3:

The Poinsettia Star block starts out as one of our main star blocks. Next, we add a row to all four sides, using Option #3 Flying Geese, with a rectangle and a solid square unit. Watch for color placement on the Option #3, as well as special trimming instructions to keep the color where you need it.

Hint: When cutting the rectangles, cut the strip the small number and crosscut the strip for the longer number.

Hint: Remember, sewn-finished and graph paper size is smaller than the cut or raw edge size of a unit or complete block.

The fabric amounts listed below will yield approximately (12) Poinsettia Star Blocks.

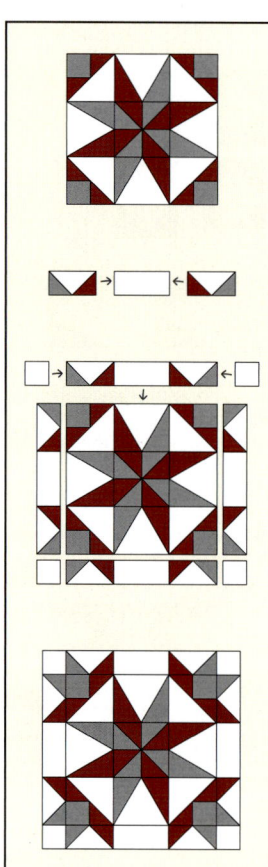

Block Size:	9 ½" cut, 9" sewn	
Main Star: Cut 8" – Sewn 7 ½"		
Fabric 1		4 ⅝" center square for Option #4 pinwheel
		1 ⅞" surround strips for Option #18, opposite sides
		3 ¼" center square for Option #11
		1 ½" surround strips for Option #3, 2 sides
Fabric 2		2 ½" surround strips for Option #4 pinwheel
		1 ⅞" surround strips for Option #18, opposite sides
		2" surround strips for row one, Option #11
		1 ½" surround strips for Option #3, 2 sides
Fabric 3		3 ¼" center diamond for Option #18, 2 needed per block
		2 ¾" surround strips for row two, Option #11
		2 ⅜" center squares for Option #3, 4 needed per block
		1 ⅝" x 3" rectangles, 4 needed per block
		1 ⅝" corner squares, 4 needed per block
Fabric		1 ¼ yd Fabric 1
		1 ¾ yd Fabric 2
		1 ¾ yd Fabric 3

Block Size:	13" cut, 12 ½" sewn
Main Star:	Cut 10" – Sewn 9 ½"

Fabric 1	5 ½" center square for Option #4 pinwheel
	2 ⅛" surround strips for Option #18, opposite sides
	4" center square for Option #11
	1 ¾" surround strips for Option #3, 2 sides
Fabric 2	3" surround strips for Option #4 pinwheel
	2 ⅛" surround strips for Option #18, opposite sides
	2 ¼" surround strips for row one, Option #11
	1 ¾" surround strips for Option #3, 2 sides
Fabric 3	3 ¾" center diamond for Option #18, 2 needed per block
	3 ¼" surround strips for row two, Option #11
	3" center squares for Option #3, 4 needed per block
	4" x 4" rectangles, 4 needed per block
	2" corner squares, 4 needed per block
Fabric	1 ½ yd Fabric 1
	2 ayd Fabric 2
	2 ½ yd Fabric 3

Block Size:	15" cut, 14 ½" sewn
Main Star:	Cut 11 ½" – Sewn 11"

Fabric 1	6 ⅛" center square for Option #4 pinwheel
	2 ⅜" surround strips for Option #18, opposite sides
	4 ½" center square for Option #11
	2" surround strips for Option #3, 2 sides
Fabric 2	3 ½" surround strips for Option #4 pinwheel
	2 ⅜" surround strips for Option #18, opposite sides
	2 ½" surround strips for row one, Option #11
	2" surround strips for Option #3, 2 sides
Fabric 3	4 ¼" center diamond for Option #18, 2 needed per block
	3 ½" surround strips for row two, Option #11
	3 ⅜" center squares for Option #3, 4 needed per block
	2 ¼" x 4 ½" rectangles, 4 needed per block
	2 ¼" corner squares, 4 needed per block
Fabric	1 ¾ yd Fabric 1
	2 ½ yd Fabric 2
	2 ¾ yd Fabric 3

 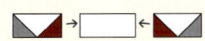 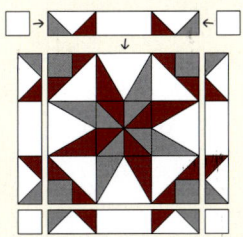 

Fringe Flower

Fringe Flower

Difficulty: Intermediate

Quilt Size: 82"x 106"

Block Size: 12 ½" cut, 12" sewn

Square in a Square® Technique: Option 18

18 Star Blocks, 17 Chain Blocks

One of my favorite settings for a quilt is a running chain through the quilt connecting the main blocks. This gives the quilt a unified design and not just a simple repeating block look.

Three additional block sizes are given at the end of this pattern.

Fabric

The following amounts are for the entire quilt.

Blue Flower: ¼ yd
Blue Paisley: 3 ½ yd
Dark Blue Linen: 2 ½ yd
Green: 3 yds
Background: 6 yds
Backing: 7 ½ yds
Binding: 1 yd

Cut

The following measurements are for cutting the entire quilt. The number in parentheses is the number of pieces that need to be cut. Strips are to be cut the full width of your fabric or selvedge to selvedge. Be sure to label and keep all of your pieces together. The numbers in the circles ❶ after each cutting, correspond with the sewing steps.

Blue Flower: ¼ yd
(2) 3 ½" strips for Irish Chain ❿

Blue Paisley: 3 ½ yd
(30) 1 ¾" surround strips for Option 18 ❶
(4) 2" strips for Irish Chain ⓫
(10) 6 ½" strips for middle border ⓰

Dark Blue Linen: 2 ½ yds
(4) 1 ¾" strips for 3-Patch unit ❷
(2) 3 ½" strips into (22) 3" squares for center of blocks ❾
(4) 2" strips for Irish Chain ⓬
(10) 3" strips for outer border ⓰

Green: 3 yds
(10) 1 ¾" strips for 3-Patch unit ❷
(8) 1 ¾" strips into (72) 1 ¾" x 3" rectangles ❷
Hint: leave in a long strip for strip piecing
(8) 2" strips for Irish Chain ❾
(9) 3 ½" strips for inner border ⓰

Background: 6 yds
(8) 2 ⅞" strip into (72) 2 ⅞" center diamonds for Option 18 ❶
(7) 2 ¾" strips into (72) 2 ¾" corner squares ❸
(12) 3" strips into (72) 3" x 5 ¼" setting rectangles ❻❼
(4) 3 ½" strips for Irish Chain ❾
(4) 2" strips for Irish Chain ❿
(2) 6 ½" strips for Irish Chain ⓫
(2) 9 ½" strips for Irish Chain ⓬
(6) 6 ½" strip into (36) 2" x 6 ½" rectangles for Irish Chain ⓮
(2) 9 ½" strips into (36) 2" x 9 ½" rectangles for Irish Chain ⓯

Sew

1. Sew and cut (72) Option 18s using 2 ⅞" center diamonds from background and 1 ¾" surround strips from blue paisley.
2. Strip piece 1 ¾" green strips and 1 ¾" dark blue strips. Crosscut into 1 ¾" 2-Patch units.
   Strip piece 1 ¾" green strip to the long side of the 2-Patch. Cut apart, squaring up and press to the rectangle unit. Repeat for a total of (72) 3-Patch units.
3. Sew (1) 2 ¾" corner square from background to (1) Option 18 Canadian Goose from step 1.
4. Sew (1) 3-Patch unit from step 2 to (1) Option 18 Canadian Goose from step 1. Watch color placement.
5. Sew (1) unit from step 3 and (1) unit from step 4 together. Repeat for a total of (72) units.
6. Sew (2) units from step 5 to (1) 3" x 5 ¼" rectangle from background. Repeat for a total of (36) sections.
7. Sew (2) 3" x 5 ¼" rectangles from background to (1) 3" square from dark blue. Repeat for a total of (18) sections.
8. Sew (2) sections from step 6 to (1) section from step 7. Repeat for a total of (18) quilt blocks.
9. Sew (1) 3 ½" strip from background between (2) 2" strips from green. Strip piece four separate stratas and cross cut into 2" units. Repeat for a total of (68) units.
10. Sew (1) 3 ½" strip from blue flower between (2) 2" strips from background. Strip piece two separate stratas and cross cut into 3 ½" units. Repeat for a total of (17) units.
11. Sew (1) 6 ½" strip from background between (2) 2" strips from blue paisley. Strip piece two separate stratas and cross cut into 2" units. Repeat for a total of (34) units.
12. Sew (1) 9 ½" strip from background between (2) 2" strips from dark blue. Strip piece two seperate stratas and cross cut into 2" units. Repeat for a total of (34) units.

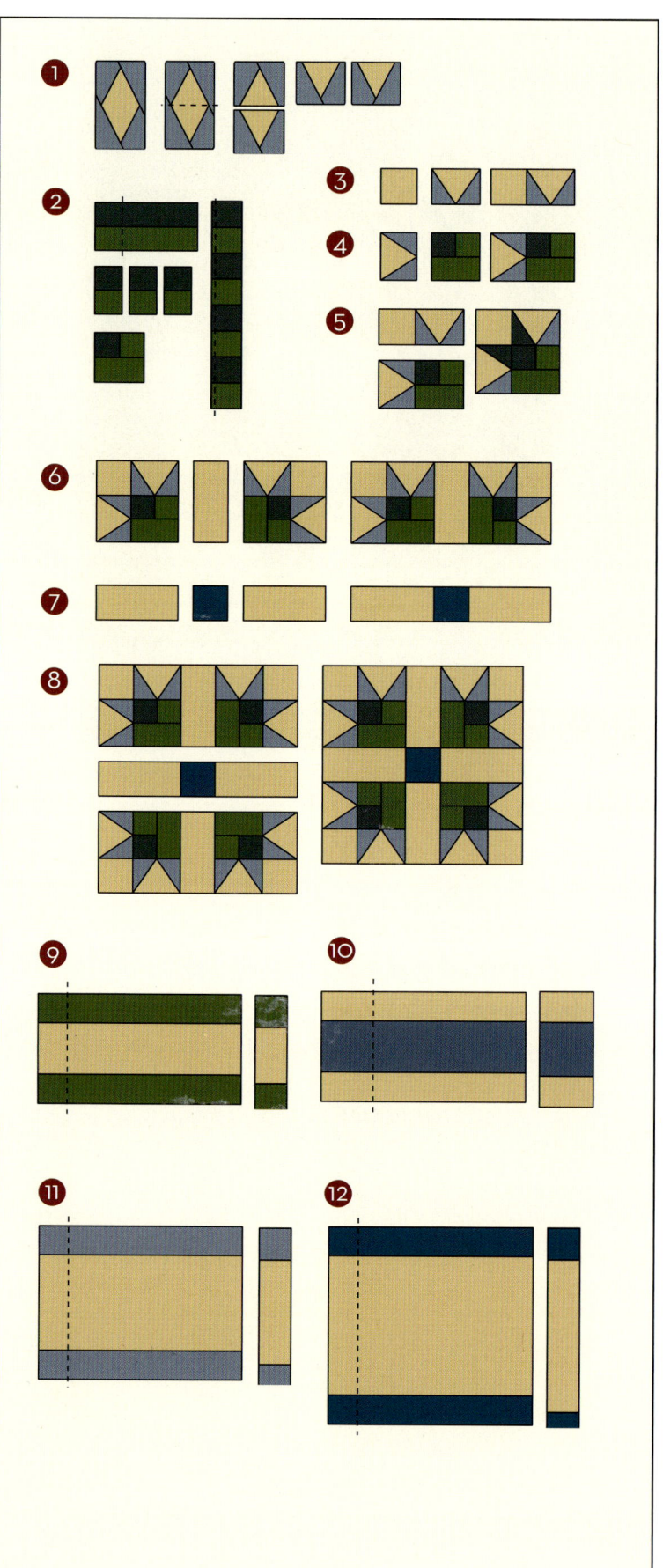

13. Sew (1) unit from step 10 between (2) units from step 9. Repeat for a total of (17) units.
14. Sew (1) unit from step 13 between (2) 2" x 6 ½" rectangles from background. Sew (2) units from step 11 on the other two sides. Repeat for a total of (17) sections.
15. Sew (1) section from step 14 between (2) 2" x 9 ½" rectangles from background. Sew (2) units from step 12 on the other two sides. Repeat for a total of (17) blocks. Sew alternating blocks from Step 8 and Step 15 together in rows. Sew four (4) rows using the Step 8 block first and three (3) rows using the Step 15 block first.
16. Sew 3 ½" strips from green for the inner border into long strips.
Sew the long side of the border to the quilt first, then add the top and bottom. Repeat with the 6 ½" strips from blue paisley for the middle border.
Repeat with the 3" strips from dark blue for the outer border.

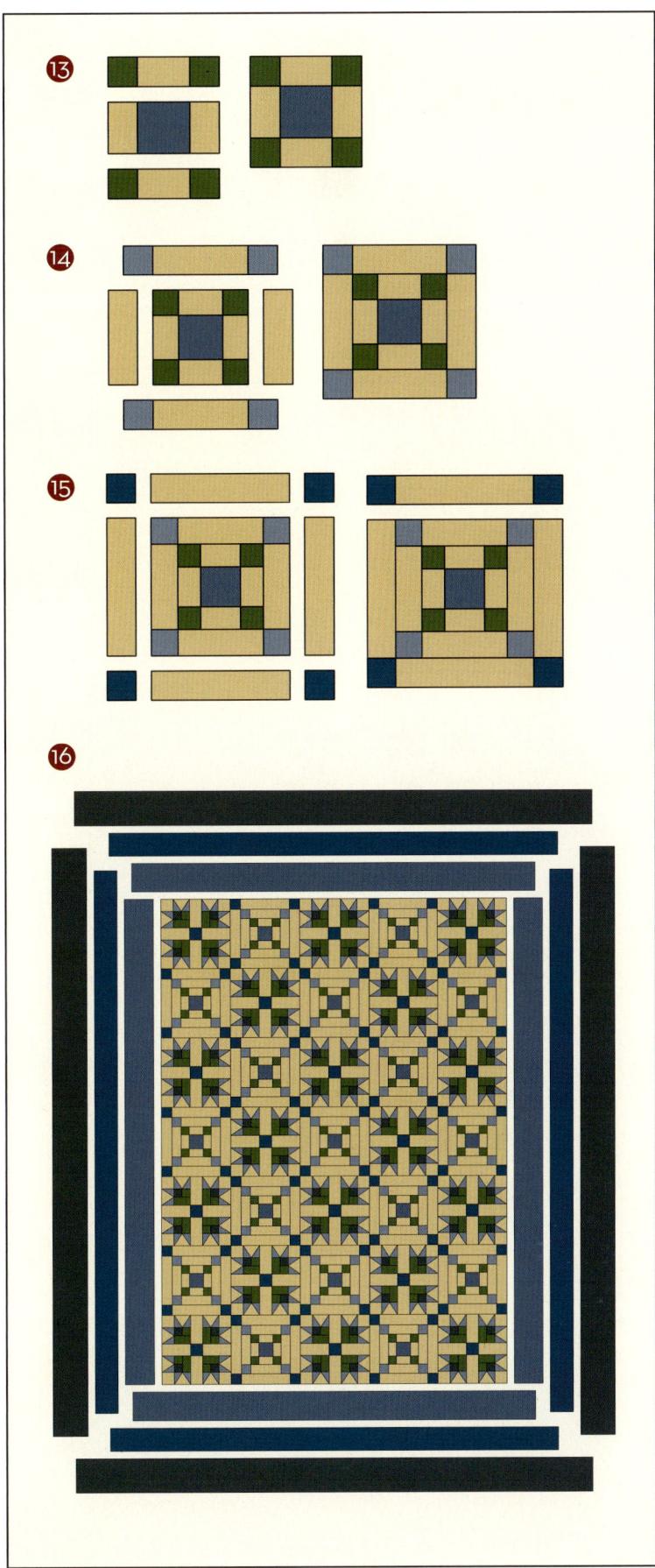

Fringe Flower Variations

Fabric 1:   Fabric 2:

Fabric 3:   Fabric 4:

The Fringe Flower block can be sewn in multiple block sizes. For different size you can also refer to the Option 18 Chart at the front of the book. We've done the work for you for three different sized blocks on this page. We have also included estimated fabric amounts per block.

To sew this block together refer to directions on the previous page.

Block Size:	6 ½" cut, 6" sewn
Corner Squares	(1) 1 ½" cut strip yields 6 blocks totaling (26) **corner squares** [⅛ yd yields 12 blocks]
	(4) corner squares required per block
Rectangle	(1) 2 ¾" cut strip cross cut into 2" x 2 ¾" **rectangles** yields 5 blocks totaling (20) rectangles [¼ yd yields 15 blocks]
	(4) rectangles required per block
Center Square	(1) 2" cut strip yields 20 blocks totaling (20) **center squares** [⅛ yd yields 40 blocks]
	(1) center square required per block
Square – 2-Patch Unit Color A	(1) 1 ⅛" strip yields 8 blocks totaling (32) **2-Patch unit squares** [⅛ yd yields 16 blocks]
	(4) color A required per block
Square – 2-Patch Unit Color B	(1) 1 ⅛" strip yields 8 blocks totaling (32) **2-Patch unit squares** [⅛ yd yields 16 blocks]
	(4) color B required per block
Rectangle Units	(1) 1 ⅛" strip cross cut into 1 ⅛" x 2 ¾" rectangles yields 3 ½ blocks totaling (14) **rectangles** [⅛ yd yields 7 blocks]
	(4) rectangle units required per block
Option 18	(1) 1 ¾" cut strip yields (20) **center diamonds** or (40) Canadian Geese to yield 5 blocks [⅛ yd yields 10 blocks]
	(1) 1 ⅛" cut surround strip yields 5 diamond units totaling (10) **Canadian Geese** [¼ yd yields 5 blocks]
	(4) diamond units required per block

	Block Size: 8 ½" cut, 8" sewn
Corner Squares	(1) 2" cut strip yields 5 blocks totaling (20) **corner squares** [⅛ yd yields 10 blocks] (4) corner squares required per block
Rectangle	(1) 2" cut strip cross cut into 2" x 3 ¾" rectangles yields 2 blocks totaling (10) **rectangles** [⅛ yd yields 4 blocks] (4) rectangle units required per block
Center Square	(1) 2" cut strip yields 20 blocks totaling (20) **center squares** [⅛ yd yields 40 blocks] (1) center square required per block
Square – 2-Patch Unit Color A	(1) 1 ⅜" strip yields 6 blocks totaling (26) **2-Patch unit squares** [⅛ yd yields 13 blocks] (4) color A required per block
Square – 2-Patch Unit Color B	(1) 1 ⅜" strip yields 6 blocks totaling (26) **2-Patch unit squares** [⅛ yd yields 13 blocks] (4) color B required per block
Rectangle Units	(1) 1 ⅜" strip cross cut into 1 ⅜" x 2 ¼" rectangles yields 4 blocks totaling (17) **rectangles** [⅛ yd yields 8 blocks] (4) rectangle units required per block
Option 18	(1) 2 ¼" cut strip yields (16) **center diamonds** or (32) Canadian Geese to yield 4 blocks [⅛ yd yields 15 blocks] (1) 1 ⅜" cut surround strip yields 3 diamond units totaling (6) **Canadian Geese** [⅛ yd yields 3 blocks] (4) diamond units required per block

	Block Size: 9 ½" cut, 9" sewn
Corner Squares	(1) 2 ¼" cut strip yields 4 blocks totaling (17) **corner squares** [⅛ yd yields 8 blocks] (4) corner squares required per block
Rectangle	(1) 2" cut strip cross cut into 2" x 4 ¼" rectangles yields 2 blocks totaling (9) **rectangles** [¼ yd yields 8 blocks] (4) rectangles required per block
Center Square	(1) 2" cut strip yields 20 blocks totaling (20) **center squares** [⅛ yd yields 40 blocks] (1) center square required per block
Square – 2-Patch Unit Color A	(1) 1 ½" strip yields 6 blocks totaling (26) **2-Patch unit squares** [⅛ yd yields 12 blocks] (4) color A required per block
Square – 2-Patch Unit Color B	(1) 1 ½" strip yields 6 blocks totaling (26) **2-Patch unit squares** [⅛ yd yields 12 blocks] (4) color B required per block
Rectangle Units	(1) 1 ½" strip cross cut into 1 ½" x 2 ½" rectangles yields 4 blocks totaling (16) **rectangles** [⅛ yd yields 8 blocks]
Option 18	(1) 2 ½" cut strip yields (13) **center diamonds** or (26) Canadian Geese units to yield 18 blocks [¼ yd yields 18 blocks] (2) 1 ½" cut **surround strips** yields 6 diamond units or (12) **Canadian Geese** to yield 1 ½ blocks [¼ yd yields 8 blocks] (4) diamond units required per block

Star Frost

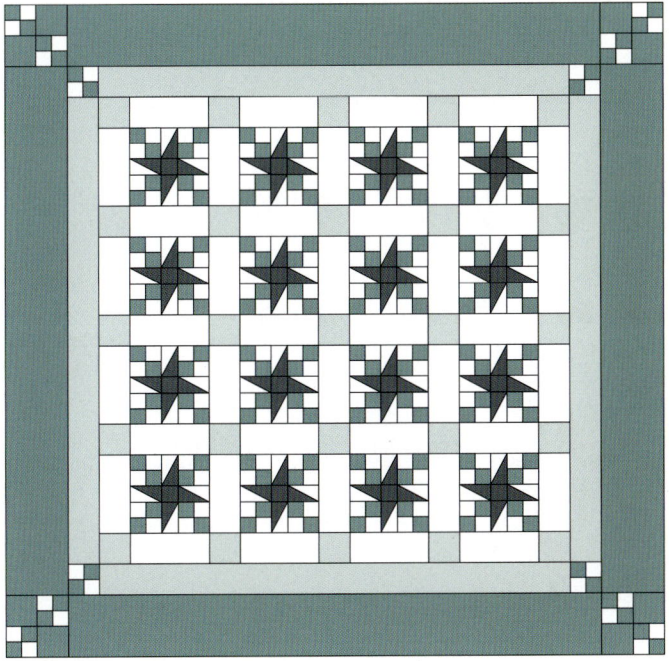

Star Frost

Difficulty: Intermediate

Quilt Size: 64"x 76"

Block Size: 8 ½" cut, 7 ¾" sewn

Square in a Square® Technique: Option 19

Star Frost is a beautiful star quilt. Option 19 results in four long, thin "half-square triangles." Because two of the units are mirror images of each other, half the stars in this quilt twists to the left and the other half twists to the right.

Three additional block sizes are given at the end of this pattern.

Fabric

The following amounts are for the entire quilt.

Background: 2 ¾ yds
Dark Floral Print: 2 ½ yds
Dark Blue Print: ½ yd
Icy Blue Print: ¾ yd
Backing: 5 yds
Binding: 1 yd

Cut

The following measurements are for cutting the entire quilt. The number in parentheses is the number of pieces that need to be cut. Strips are to be cut the full width of your fabric or selvedge to selvedge. Be sure to label and keep all of your pieces together. The numbers in the circles ❶ after each cutting, correspond with the sewing steps.

Background: 4 yds
(10) 2" strips for (4) 4-Patch units ❶
(11) 2 ½" surround strips for Option 19 ❷
(13) 3 ½" strips into (49) 3 ½" x 8 ¼" rectangles for sashing ❺ ❻

Dark Floral Print: 2 ½ yds
(10) 2" strips for 4-Patch units ❶
(4) 3 ½" strips into (38) 3 ½" squares for cornerstone and outside corner blocks.
(7) 6 ½" strips for outer border ❽

Dark Blue Print: ½ yd
(3) 4 ¼" strips into (20) 4 ¼" diamonds for Option 19 ❷

Icy Blue Print: ¾ yd
(2) 2 ¼" strips into (20) 2 ¼" solid squares for star centers ❸
(5) 3 ½" strips for inner border ❼

Sew

1. Sew (5) stratas using 2" strips of background and dark blue print for 4-Patch units. Cross-cut into 2" segments. Sew 4-Patch blocks together. Repeat for a total of (92) 4-Patches.
2. Sew and cut (20) Option 19s using 4 ¼" dark blue diamonds and 2 ½" surround strips from background.
3. Sew each block together using (4) Option 19s from Step 2 and (4) 4-Patch units from Step 1 and (1) 2" square for star center. Repeat for a total of (20) blocks.
   Hint: Watch placement of the mirror image units carefully in order to have the correct twist to the stars.
4. Sew (4) completed blocks from Step 3 together in a row, alternating with 3 ½" x 8 ¼" setting rectangles from background. Repeat for a total of (5) rows.
   Hint: Watch placement for alternating twist of stars.
5. Sew (5) 3 ½" setting squares from dark floral alternating with (4) 3 ½" x 8 ¼" sashing rectangles from background. Repeat for a total of (6) rows.
   Sew the rows of Step 4 and Step 5 together, alternating rows. The finished quilt will be (4) rows across and (6) rows down.
6. Sew the rows of Step 4 and Step 5 together, alternating rows. The finished quilt will be (4) rows across and (6) rows down.
7. Sew 3 ½" border strips from Icy Blue on two sides of the quilt top. Sew a 4-Patch block to each end of the other two border strips and sew to the quilt.
8. Sew 6 ½" border strips to two sides of the quilt top. Sew (1) double 4-Patch block with (2) 3 ½" Dark Blue squares. Repeat for a total of (4) blocks. Sew (1) double 4-Patch block to each end of the other two 6 ½" border strips and sew to the quilt.

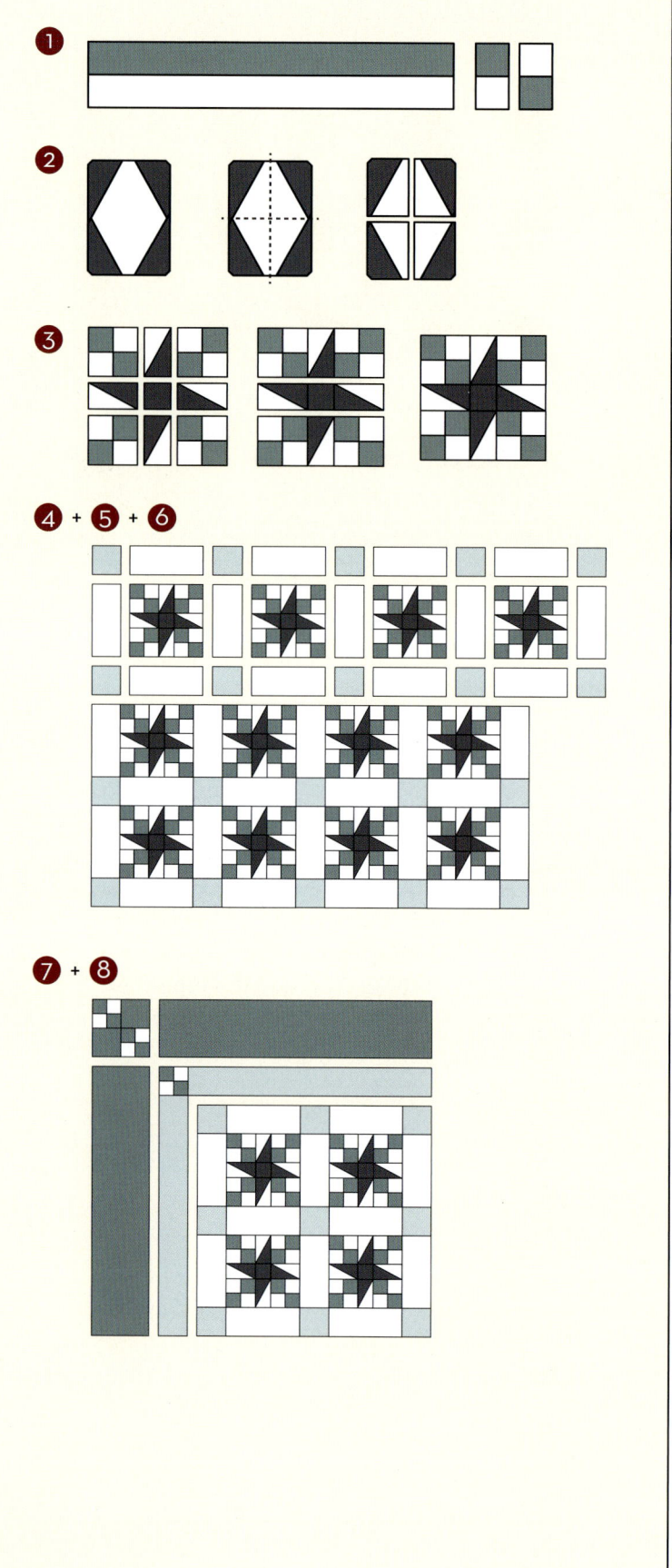

112

Star Frost Variations

Fabric 1:

Fabric 2:

Fabric 3:

The Star Frost block can be sewn in multiple block sizes. For a different size refer to the 4-Patch and Option 19 Charts at the front of the book. We've done the work for you for the three different sized blocks on this page. We have also included estimated fabric amounts per block.

To sew this block together, refer to directions on the previous page.

Block Size:	3 ½" cut, 3" sewn
Center Square	(1) 1 ⅛" cut strip yields 32 blocks totaling (32) **center units**
	(1) center square required per block
4-Patch	(1) 1" cut strip of color A yields 40 squares totaling (20) **4-Patch units** or 5 blocks [¼ yd yields 30 blocks]
	(1) 1" cut strip of color B yields 40 squares totaling (20) **4-Patch units** or 5 blocks [¼ yd yields 30 blocks]
	(4) 4-Patch units required per block
Option 19	(1) 2 ¼" cut strip yields (14) **center diamonds** or 7 star blocks twisting left and 7 star blocks twisting right totaling 12 blocks [⅛ yd yields 14 blocks of right twist and 14 blocks of left twist]
	(1) 1 ⅜" cut **surround strip** yields 4 diamond units totaling 4 blocks [⅛ yd yields 8 blocks]

Block Size:	4 ½" cut, 4" sewn
Center Square	(1) 1 ⅜" cut strip yields 26 blocks totaling (26) **center units**
	(1) center square required per block
4-Patch	(1) 1 ¼" cut strip of color A yields 32 squares totaling (16) **4-Patch units** or 5 blocks [¼ yd yields 24 blocks]
	(1) 1 ¼" cut strip of color B yields 32 squares totaling (16) **4-Patch units** or 5 blocks [¼ yd yields 24 blocks]
	(4) 4-Patch units required per block
Option 19	(1) 2 ⅞" cut strip yields (9) **center diamonds** or 4 star blocks twisting left and 4 star blocks twisting right [⅛ yd yields 9 blocks of right twist and 9 blocks of left twist]
	(1) 1 ¾" cut **surround strip** yields 2 diamond units totaling 2 blocks [⅛ yd yields 4 blocks]

Block Size:	7 ½" cut, 7" sewn
Center Square	(1) 2 ⅛" cut strip yields 17 blocks totaling (17) center units
	(1) center square required per block
4-Patch	(1) 1 ⅞" cut strip of color A yields 20 squares totaling (10) **4-Patch units** or 2.5 blocks [¼ yd yields 3 blocks]
	(1) 1 ⅞" cut strip of color B yields 20 squares totaling (10) **4-Patch units** or 2.5 blocks [¼ yd yields 3 blocks]
	(4) 4-Patch units required per block
Option 19	(1) 4" cut strip yields (8) **center diamonds** or 4 star blocks twisting left and 6 star blocks twisting right totaling 8 blocks [¼ yd yields 8 blocks right twist and 8 blocks left twist]
	(1) 2 ¼" cut **surround strip** yields 1.5 diamond units totaling 1.5 blocks [¼ yard yields 5 blocks]

Pathway to the Stars

Pathway to the Stars

Difficulty: Intermediate
Quilt Size: 52"x 61"
Block Size: 7 ½" cut, 7" sewn
Block Quantity: 22
Square in a Square® Technique: Option 29

Fabric
The following amounts are for the entire quilt.
2 fat quarters each of gold, green, red, black and brown: 10 fat quarters total
8 fat quarters tan or background muted tones.
Centers, Sashings, Borders: 3 ½ yds
Gold Border: ½ yd
Green Star for Border: 1 ½ yds
Black Plaid Backing: 4 yds
Red with Gold Star Binding: 1 yd

Cut
The following measurements are for cutting the entire quilt. The number in parentheses is the number of pieces that need to be cut. Strips are to be cut the full width of your fabric or selvedge to selvedge. Be sure to label and keep all of your pieces together. The numbers in the circles ❶ after each cutting, correspond with the sewing steps.

2 fat quarters each of gold, green, red, black and brown: 10 total
(30) 1 ¾" strips for Option 29, row 1 star points ❶❷
Hint: if using selvage to selvage yardage you will only need to cut (15)
(15) 2" fat quarter strips for Option 29, 2 sides of row 2 ❶❷
(3) 1 ¾" fat quarter strips of black for Option 29, border star point, row 1 ❷
(2) 8" squares from red fat quarter and slice into 4 triangle units ❹

8 fat quarters tan or background muted tones
(2) 7 ½" strips into (6) setting squares ❸
(9) 3" strips into (21) 3" x 7 ½" sashings ❸
Hint: if you use the leftovers from the setting squares, you may not need these 9 strips—you may only need (2) strips of the muted background colors
(7) 3" strips into (50) 3" diamond centers for Option 29 and border stars ❶❷
(26) 3 ¼" fat quarter strips for Option 29, 2 sides of row 2 ❶❷

Background: 3 ½" yds

Centers, Sashings, Borders:
(3) 2 ½" strips sewn into (2) 2 ½" x 49 ½" for side border units ❸

Gold Border: ½ yd
(7) 1 ½" strips for outer border 1 ❹

Green Star for Border: 1 ½ yds
(2) 5 ½" x approx 40 ½" for top and bottom borders ❹
(3) 5 ½" x approx 49 ½" for side borders ❹
Hint: measure your quilt exactly before cutting the borders.

Sew

1. Sew and cut (44) Option 29s using 3" center diamonds from muted background colors and 1 ¾" surround strips for row 1 from red, gold, brown, green and black. These will be your star points.
   For row 2, short sides (60° points) of the center diamond, sew 2" surround strips from the dark colors.
   For row 2, long sides (120° points) of the center diamond, sew 3 ¼" surround strips from muted background colors.
   Hint: watch your trimming on this Option. Sew the Star together. Repeat for (22) blocks.

2. For the border stars:
   Sew and cut (6) Option 29s using 3" center diamonds from muted background colors and 1 ¾" surround strips from black for row 1. These will be your star points.
   On (4) options, for row 2, short sides (60° points) of the center diamond, sew 2" surround strips from red.
   On (2) options, for row 2, short sides (60° points) of the center diamond, sew 2" surround strips from black.
   On all (6) options, for row 2, long sides (120° points) of the center diamond sew 3 ¼" surround strips from background colors. Sew together as shown.

3. Sew the quilt top together in vertical rows using the 3" x 7 ½" background sashing and (6) 7 ½" setting squares.
   Sew (1) 2 ½" background strip to the left and right side of the pieced quilt.
   Sew the star points from step 2 to the 5 ½" corner border sections.

4. Measure the length and width of the sewn quilt top. Sew the red triangles across the ends of the 5 ½" wide border sections. Pay careful attention to the direction or placement of the angle. Double check before you sew. Trim the red triangles on the border after it is sewn. Sew the (4) gold border lengths to the quilt.

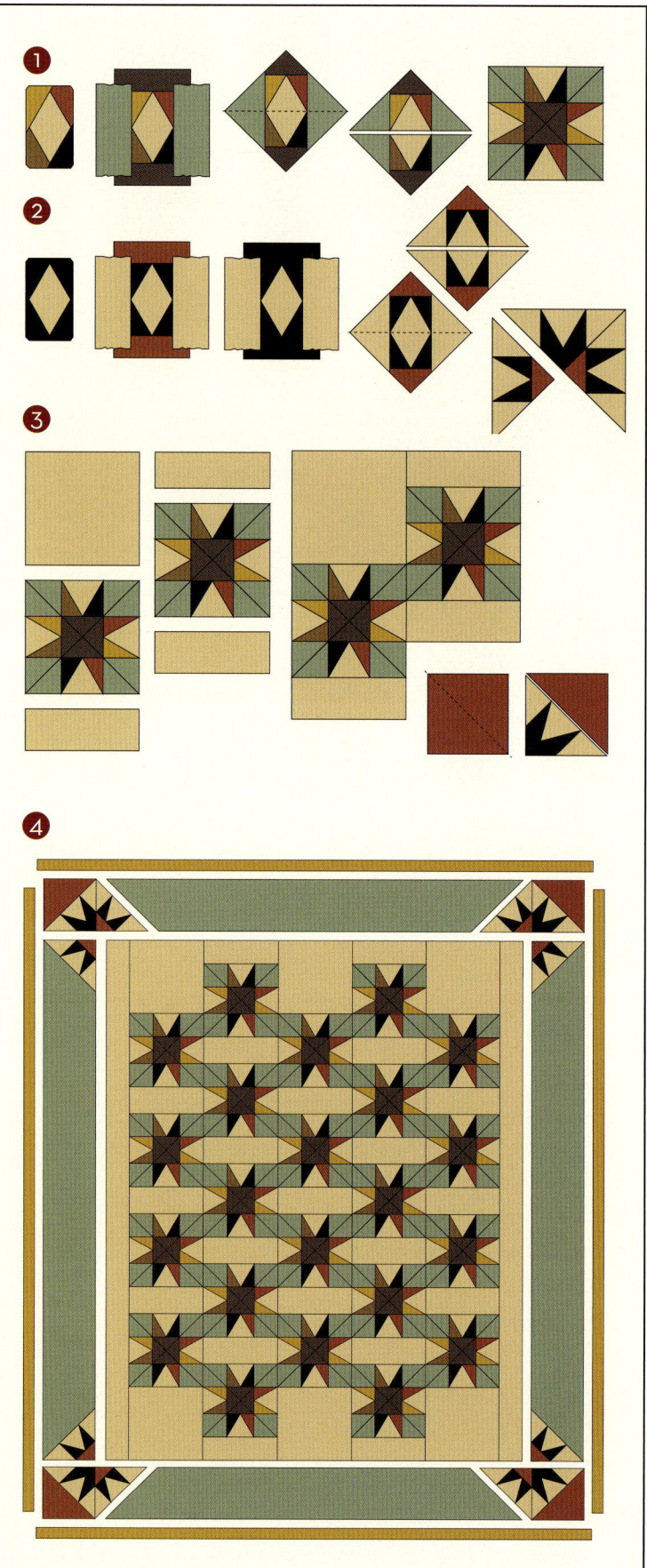

Crown of Thorns

Crown of Thorns

Difficulty: Intermediate
Quilt Size: 52"x 52"
Block Size: 14" cut, 13 ½" sewn
Square in a Square® Technique: Option 30

Option 30, "Father Goose" is an awesome triangle unit. Not only does it make the star points, but the large outside triangles create a graceful, twisting ribbon effect when used in the border. This triangle system continues to inspire and opens the door of opportunity to the average quilter.

Fabric
The following amounts are for the entire quilt.
Blue 1: ⅓ yd
Blue 2: ⅛ yd
Blue 3: 1 yd
Red: 1 ¼ yd
Brown: ½ yd
Green: ½ yd
Cream: 1 ½ yds
Backing: 3 ½ yds
Binding: ¾ yd

Cut
The following measurements are for cutting the entire quilt. The number in parentheses is the number of pieces that need to be cut. Strips are to be cut the full width of your fabric or selvedge to selvedge. Be sure to label and keep all of your pieces together. The numbers in the circles ❶ after each cutting, correspond with the sewing steps.

Blue 1: ⅓ yd
(5) 2" strips for Option 30 Row 2 surround strips ❶

Blue 2: ⅛ yd
(1) 1 ⅝" strips for small 9-Patch ❸
(1) 2 ⅝" strip for large 9-Patch ❹

Blue 3: 1 yd
(4) 4 ⅛" strips for inner border ❽
(5) 1 ½" strips for outer border ❽

Red: 1 ¼ yd
(14) 3" strips for Option 30 Row 3 surround strips ❶

Brown: ½ yd
(2) 1 ⅝" for small 9-Patch ❷
(2) 2 ⅝" strips for large 9-Patch ❹

Green: ½ yd
(7) 1 ¾" strips for Option 30 Row 1 surround strips ❶
(1) 3 ⅛" strips for large 9-Patch ❹

Cream: 1 ½ yds
(2) 3" strips into (24) 3" diamond centers for Option 30 ❶
(8) 2 ¾" strips for Option 30 Row 2 surround strips ❶
(4) 1 ⅝" strips for small 9-Patch ❷❸
(1) 3 ⅛" strips for large 9-Patch ❹
(2) 2 ⅝" strips for large 9-Patch ❹

Hint: In our quilt we put blue and green centers in the large 9-Patch. Feel free to scrap yours up.

Sew

1. Sew and cut (24) Option 30s using 3" center diamonds from cream and 1 ¾" surround strips from green. Use 2" surround strips from blue #1 on the short side of the rectangle and 2 ¾" surround strips from cream on the long side of the rectangle. Use 3" surround strips from red for Row 3. *Hint*: Watch carefully how you trim each side of each row. Repeat for a total of (48) "Father Goose" units.

2. Sew a 1 ⅝" strip from brown to both sides of a 1 ⅝" strip from cream. Repeat for (2) stratas. Cross cut the strata into 1 ⅝" units. Repeat for a total of (40) units.

3. Sew a 1 ⅝" strip from cream to both sides of a 1 ⅝" strip from blue 2. Sew (1) strata. Cross-cut the strata into 1 ⅝" units. Repeat for a total of (20) units. Sew (20) 9-Patch blocks.

4. Sew a 2 ⅝" strip from brown to both sides of a 3 ⅛" strip from cream. Repeat for (2) stratas. Use the 9-Patch ruler to cross cut the strata into 2 ⅝" units. Repeat for a total of (18) units. Sew 2 ⅝" strip from cream to both sides of a 3 ⅛" strip of green. Sew (1) strata. Use the 9-Patch ruler to cross cut into 3 ⅛" units. Repeat for a total of (9) units. Sew (9) 9-Patch blocks. *Hint:* The 3 ⅛" sections are the centers of the 9-Patch blocks.

5. Sew (4) "Father Goose" units from Step 1 and (4) small 9-Patch units from Step 3 and (1) large 9-Patch unit from Step 4 together. Repeat for a total of (4) blocks.

6. Sew (2) "Father Goose" units from Step 1 together with (1) large 9-Patch block from Step 3. Repeat for a total of (4) setting blocks.

7. Sew the quilt together using the (4) blocks from Step 5 with the (4) blocks from Step 6 and (1) 9-Patch block.

8. Sew 4 ⅛" strips from blue 3 for the inner border on all four sides. Sew (4) rows of (6) "Father Goose" units together. Sew two border rows to two opposite sides of the quilt. Sew (1) 9-Patch unit to each end of the remaining two borders and sew to the other two sides of the quilt.
Sew (5) 1 ½" strips of blue 3 together for the narrow outside border.

Sassafras Tea

Sassafras Tea

Difficulty: Intermediate
Quilt Size: 62"x 62"
Block Size: 11 ½" cut, 11" sewn
Square in a Square® Technique: Option 35

This is a fun, scrappy quilt. Directions are written to set the blocks on point but it would also be beautiful set in traditional rows. Different color placement can accent different parts of the star. Solid setting blocks are a great place to highlight your quilting skills. Have fun with this unique block and Option 35.

Hint: Refer to the Finishing Section on page 6 for instructions on setting blocks on point. Step 4 of this pattern requires this information.

Fabric

The following amounts are for the entire quilt.
Medium to Dark Pinks: 12 fat quarters
Dark Browns: 12 fat quarters
Light to Tan Creams: 12 fat quarters
Brown Setting Triangles: 1 ½ yds
Pink: ½ yd
Brown: 1 yd
Backing: 4 yds
Binding: ½ yd

Cut

The following measurements are for cutting the entire quilt. The number in parentheses is the number of pieces that need to be cut. Strips are to be cut the full width of your fabric or selvedge to selvedge. Be sure to label and keep all of your pieces together. The numbers in the circles ❶ after each cutting, correspond with the sewing steps.

Creams: Fat Quarters
(1) 3" strip from each of the 12 fat quarters into 3" center diamonds for a total of (36) center diamonds
(2) 2 ½" surround strip from each of the 12 fat quarters for Row 2 long side
(1) 1 ¾" surround strip from each of the 12 fat quarters for Row 2 short side ❶

Pink: Fat Quarters
(1) 1 ¾" surround strip from each of the 12 fat quarters for Row 1
(3) 3 ¼" surround strips from each of the 12 fat quarters for Row 3 ❶

Brown: Fat Quarters
(1) 1 ¾" surround strip from each of the 12 fat quarters for Row 1
(3) 3 ¼" surround strips from each of the 12 fat quarters for Row 3 ❶

Brown: Setting Triangles
(2) 18" squares for side setting triangles
(4) 11 ½" squares for setting squares
(2) 9" squares for corner triangles ❶

Pink: Inner Border
(6) 2 ½" strips ❶

Brown: Outer Border
(6) 5 ½" strips ❶

Sew

Each star block uses four Option #35s. You may sew the star together for two different versions. *Hint:* Mirror image units are kitty-corner of each other. A & D are the same unit and B & C are the same. Don't get frustrated, just have a great time playing with the blocks.

❶ Sew and cut (18) Option 35s using 3" center diamonds from various creams and 1 ¾" surround strips from various pinks for Row 1. Use 1 ¾" surround strips from various creams for short side of Row 2 and 2 ½" surround strips from various creams for long side of Row 2. Use 3 ¼" surround strips from various browns for Row 3.

❷ Sew and cut (18) Option 35s using 3" center diamonds from various creams and 1 ¾" surround strips from various browns for Row 1. Use 1 ¾" surround strips from various creams for short side of Row 2 and 2 ½" surround strips from various creams for long side of Row 2. Use 3 ¼" surround strips from various pinks for Row 3.

❸ From Step 1, take 2 mirror image units with pink on Row 3 from (4) of the Option 35s and from Step 2, take 2 mirror image units with brown on Row 3 from (4) of the Option 35s to make (1) star block. Repeat for a total of 9 star blocks.

❹ Cut (8) side setting triangles from (2) 18" brown squares. Cut (4) corner triangles from (2) 9" brown squares.

❺ Set the blocks on point, alternating 11 ½" pieced blocks from Step 3 with 11 ½" setting blocks. Place the (8) brown side setting triangles from step 4 on both ends of each row with the straight of grain edge to the outside of the quilt top, then add the (4) brown corner triangles from Step 4.

❻ Sew 2 ½" strips pink into long strips for the inner border. Sew the long sides to the quilt first, then add the top and bottom. Repeat for outer border, using 5 ½" strips from brown.

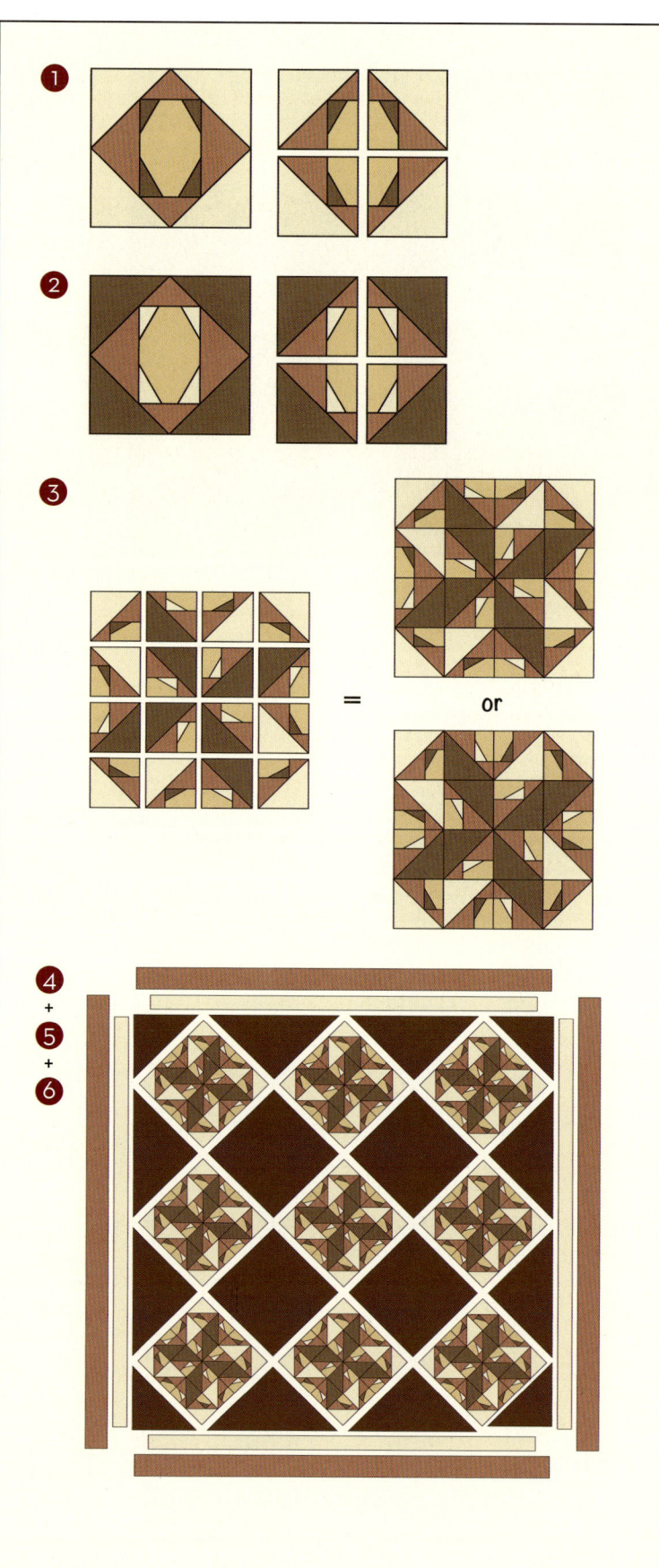

122

Kaleidoscope

Kaleidoscope

Difficulty: Intermediate

Quilt Size: 70"x 90"

Square in a Square® Technique: Options 4, 7, 18 and 4-Patch

This pattern is a row by row design. By combining a simple 4-Patch with a pinwheel and dropping in the magnificent Option 7, we create a stunning design! Don't be afraid to use scraps, batiks, or any fabric choice. The diamond units of the Square in a Square system will simplify yet another stellar quilt.

Hint: Depending on your personal private measurements (PPM), you may need to slightly trim your Option 4 pinwheel units. Sew a test pinwheel. They should measure to a cut size of 5 ¾" and match to your Option 7s from Step 3.

Fabric

The following amounts are for the entire quilt.

Assorted Scrap Fabric: ⅔ yd (4-Patch)
Assorted Mediums: 2 ½ yds
Light: 2 ¼ yds
Assorted Darks: 2 ¾ yds
Inner Border: ⅔ yd
Middle Border: 2 yds
Outer Border: ¾ yd
Backing: 6 yds
Binding: 1 yd

Cut

The following measurements are for cutting the entire quilt. The number in parentheses is the number of pieces that need to be cut. Strips are to be cut the full width of your fabric or selvedge to selvedge. Be sure to label and keep all of your pieces together. The numbers in the circles ❶ after each cutting, correspond with the sewing steps.

Assorted Scrap Fabric: ⅔ yd (4-Patch)
<u>Either</u> of the following:
(216) 2" squares, any color or value ❶
or
(11) 2" strips ❶ or
(22) 2" strips of fat quarter lengths ❶

Assorted Mediums: 2 ½ yds
(26) 2 ¾" surround strips for Option 4 ❷

Light: 2 ¼ yds
(6) 5" strips into (48) 5" center squares for Option 4 ❷
(10) 3 ¼" strips into (110) 3 ¼" center diamonds for Option 7 ❸ and Option 18 border stars ❹
(2) 2 ⅞" strips into (16) 2 ⅞" corner squares for border star
Hint: cut 3" and trim to fit ❹

Assorted Darks: 2 ¾ yds
(50) 2" surround strips for Option 7 ❸
(4) 3 ¼" squares for center of border stars ❹

Inner Border: ⅔ yd
(8) 2 ½" strips ❺

Middle Border: 2 yds
(8) 8" strips ❺

Outer Border: ¾ yd
(9) 2 ½" strips ❺

Sew

1. Sew 2" strips from assorted scraps together. Use the 4-Patch Ruler to cross cut the strata into 2" units. Repeat for a total of (108) units, or sew (54) scrappy 4-Patch blocks.
   Hint: If starting with (216) 2" squares, sew into (54) scrappy 4-Patch units.

2. Sew and cut (48) Option 4 half square triangles using a 5" center square from light and 2 ¾" surround strips from mediums. Sew into (48) pinwheel units.

3. Sew and cut (102) Option 7s using 3 ¼" center diamonds from light and 2" surround strips from darks.

4. Sew (9) rows together, alternating 4-Patch units from Step 1 and Option 7 horizontal units from Step 3.
   Sew (8) rows together, alternating Option 7 vertical units from Step 3 and pinwheel units from Step 2.

5. If you wish to put the star in each corner of the border, sew and cut (8) Option 18s using 3 ¼" center diamonds from light and 2" surround strips from dark.
   Cut (16) 2 ⅞" corner squares from light and (4) 3 ¼" solid squares from dark. Sew star block together for a total of (4) corner blocks.

6. Sew the 2 ½" strips for inner border into long strips. Sew the long sides of the border to the quilt first, then add the top and bottom.
   Sew the 8" strips for middle border into long strips. Sew the long side borders first. Next, measure and sew border pieced stars on both ends of the remaining border two strips.
   Sew the 2 ½" strips for outer border into long strips. Sew the long sides of the border to the quilt first, then add the top and bottom.

Spinning Stars

Spinning Stars

Difficulty: Intermediate
Quilt Size: 38"x 44"

Square in a Square® Technique: Option #35 is my favorite corner unit. It is so unique and versatile. You may use it as a corner unit, as a block, or as part of a cool border. For this quilt pattern, we used simple colors to make it easy but, as always, color play can completely change the pattern and make a totally different design. Once you get your feet wet, understanding this Option and the mirror image unit, you will become a master artist with design. I also recommend this one as a scrap buster quilt. Go ahead and raid your scrap basket while you learn this one.

Fabric

The following amounts are for the entire quilt.
Background: 1 ¼ yd
Red: 1 yd
Gold: ¾ yd
Black: 1 ½ yd
Backing: 1 ½ yds
Binding: ½ yd

Cut

The following measurements are for cutting the entire quilt. The number in parentheses is the number of pieces that need to be cut. Strips are to be cut the full width of your fabric or selvedge to selvedge. Be sure to label and keep all of your pieces together. The numbers in the circles ❶ after each cutting, correspond with the sewing steps.

Background: 1 ¼ yd
3) 3 ¼" strips into (24) 3 ¼" center diamonds ❶
(5) 1 ¾" surround strips for short sides, row 2 ❶
(8) 2 ½" surround strips for long sides, row 2 ❶

Red: 1 yd
(12) 1 ¾" surround strips for row 1 ❶
(4) 2" strips for inner border ❹

Gold: ¾ yd
(8) 3" surround strips for row 3 ❷

Black: ½ yd
(8) 3" surround strips for row 3 ❷
(4) 5" strips for outer border ❹

Sew

1. Sew and cut (24) Option 35s using 3 ¼" center diamonds from background and 1 ¾" surround strips from red for row 1. For row 2, use 1 ¾" surround strips from background on the 60° points of the center diamond and 2 ½" surround strips from background on the 120° points. Divide the blocks into 2 stacks of (12).

2. **Block A**
   For row 3, sew 3" surround strips from gold to all 4 sides.

   Block B
   For row 3, sew 3" surround strips from black to all 4 sides.

3. Sew the units together creating 12 gold and 12 black stars. Half of them will spin to the left and the other half will spin to the right. Sew in alternating colors and spin direction.

4. Sew the 2" red inner borders to the long sides first, then add the top and bottom. For the outer border, sew the 5" black into long strips. Sew the long sides of the border first, then add the top and bottom.

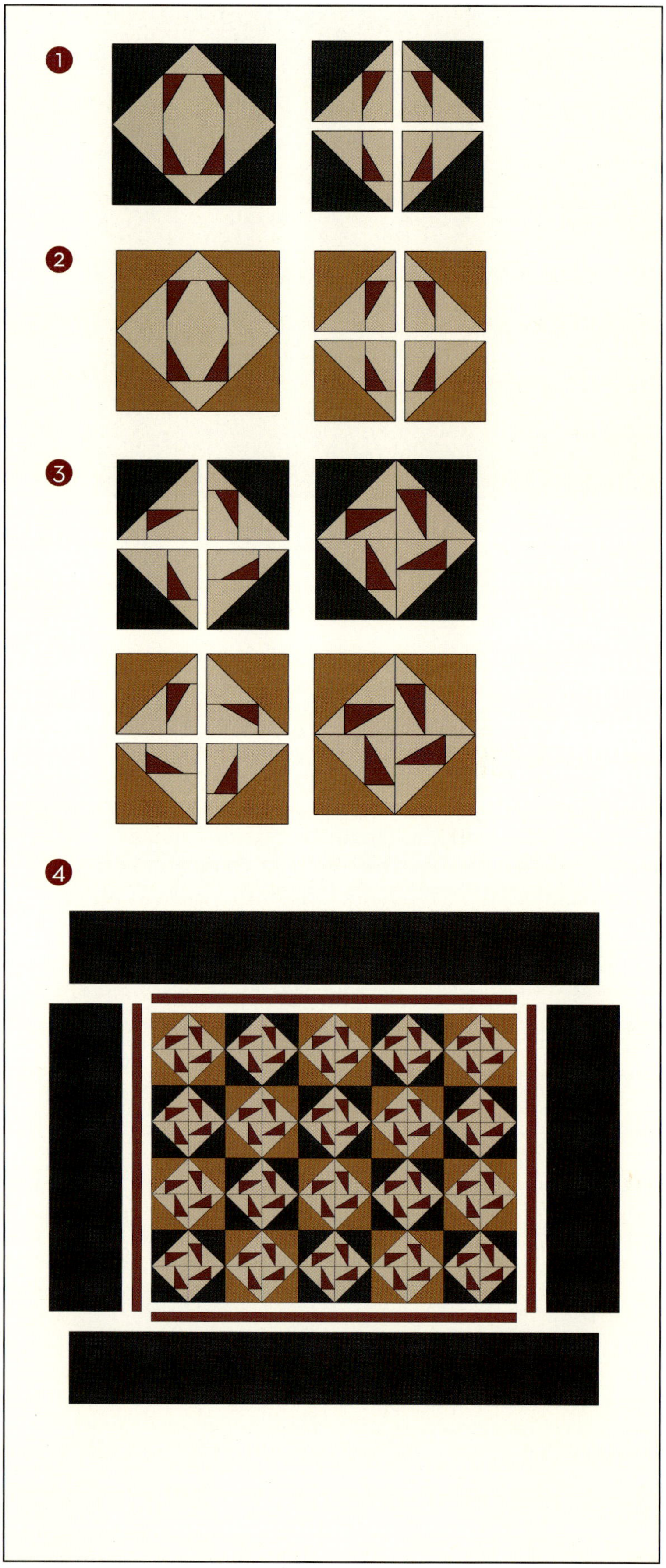